SAILOR MAN

The Troubled Life and Times
of J.P. Nunnally, USN

DEL STAECKER

HELLGATE PRESS   ASHLAND, OREGON

SAILOR MAN
©2015 Del Staecker

Published by Hellgate Press
(An imprint of L&R Publishing, LLC)

Hellgate Press
PO Box 3531
Ashland, OR 97520
email: sales@hellgatepress.com

Editor: Harley B. Patrick
Cover Design: L. Redding

Library of Congress Cataloging-in-Publication Data

Staecker, Del.
  Sailor man : the troubled life and times of J.P. Nunnally, USN / Del Staecker.
    pages cm
  ISBN 978-1-55571-816-9

1. Nunnally, J. P. (James Preston), 1926-1994. 2. World War, 1939-1945--Campaigns--Pacific Area--Personal narratives. 3. Fuller (Ship) 4. Sailors--United States--Correspondence. 5. Alcoholics--United States--Biography. 6. Post-traumatic stress disorder--Case studies. 7. Fathers and sons--United States--Biography. 8. Veterans--Mental health--United States--Case studies. 9. World War, 1939-1945--Participation, Juvenile. 10. World War, 1939-1945--Personal narratives. I. Title. II. Title: Troubled life and times of J.P. Nunnally, USN.
  D767.S73 2015
  940.54'5973092--dc23
  [B]

                        2015005470

Printed and bound in the United States of America
First Edition 10 9 8 7 6 5 4 3 2 1

This book is for all the veterans wounded by war, their families, and loved ones, and especially for J.P., Harold, and Audrey.

CONTENTS

FOREWORD

*S*AILOR *MAN* IS THE UNUSUAL AND TOUCHING STORY about a man who survived the horrors and dangers of war in the Pacific in World War II only to return home broken in spirit and an alcoholic before his twentieth birthday. The account itself is remarkable because it comes from the book's main character through a significant series of letters to his son.

After illegally enlisting in the U.S. Navy at age sixteen, the author of those letters, James P. Nunnally, found himself a crewman aboard an attack transport, a kind of mother-ship which carried troops and supplies to be off-loaded aboard landing craft in beach assaults. As a floating supply base and source of reinforcements just off the beaches under assault, an attack transport was a primary target for Japanese aircraft. The fight at sea in order to survive these attacks was about as hazardous for the crew as fighting on the beaches was for the troops which they delivered.

In these letters, we find a vivid account of crewmen burned to death, shattered by bomb fragments, and in other ways mangled. They further describe how young sailors worked feverishly to supply the beaches, recover the wounded on them, and to man the ship's antiaircraft batteries. The constant labor as well as fear often led to exhaustion and it is recalled that on one occasion the author of the letters was left to sleep peacefully through a three-hour Japanese air attack. Moreover, this kind of experience was repeated again and again as the U.S. fleet worked its way toward the Japanese homeland.

It's not surprising that many sailors turned to alcohol in their limited free time to help endure the unendurable. When allowed leave, sailor Nunnally and his fellow crew members made the local bar their first port of call and long before the war ended he was already in the advanced stages of alcoholism.

The young hero of this book remained an alcoholic to the day of his death as an elderly man, and was as much a victim of the war as any soldier or sailor who died as the result of enemy action. But before he went, he left an invaluable store of letters about one boy's experience of war.

There are many stories about the war in the Pacific; this one is about what happened to a boy's soul that put him on the road to perdition. We have Mr. Staecker to thank for presenting this thoughtful revelation about the cost of war.

—Larry H. Addington, Emeritus Professor of History,
The Citadel, The Military College of South Carolina.
Author of *The Patterns of War Since the Eighteenth Century, The Blitzkrieg Era and the German General Staff :1865-1941, America's War in Vietnam: A Short Narrative History*, and *Patterns of World War II.*

INTRODUCTION

U PON EXAMINING THE RECORDS CONCERNING World War Two's Pacific Theater, one finds no mention of James Preston Nunnally. Within those works individual seamen receive emphasis only under extraordinary and/or heroic circumstances, and, although he served ably as a crew member of the legendary attack transport U.S.S. *Fuller* (APA-7) from 1943 through the war's end and bravely participated in seven invasions, Nunnally did not distinguish himself through heroic acts notable enough to receive singular recognition. As far as the historical record is concerned Nunnally is merely one of the numerous veteran sailors who served as best they could and remained anonymous, both during and after the war.

However, the Pacific war was won by these ordinary men who enthusiastically answered the patriot call that swept the United States after December 7, 1941. And, what makes this otherwise ordinary man noteworthy is his ability late in life to simply and honestly portray his war-time experience in a series of remarkably honest letters written to the son he barely knew.

Within his personal accounts Nunnally candidly and vividly describes the dull grind of the routine at sea, the stark terror of combat, and, sadly, his reliance upon alcohol to ease his pain and to erase the memories of what he had seen and done during his transformation from a naive country boy to hardened veteran. And sadly, his letters reveal the price he paid to be a member of what has been called the greatest generation.

Nunnally, like so many young enlistees, knew very little about war. Beyond the posters and pamphlets produced to entice his service he had no idea what perils he would face in war nor what his service would cost him, the people he loved, and those who loved him. Under-aged, (he was only sixteen when he illegally enlisted) J.P., as he was known to his family and friends, was not yet twenty when he returned home at the conclusion of the war. An adolescent at its start and barely an adult at the end of his service, J.P. faced challenges beyond his abilities to interpret and cope, and ultimately to prevail, and, most sadly, to function in life upon returning home.

As a civilian, the good life of the post-war American boom evaded J.P. Nunnally. Overwhelmed by the negative elements of combat-related service in the Pacific Theater, J.P was seriously damaged by the war and further broken by well-intentioned but ineffective treatment after returning to his family and home town.

Unsuccessful in his fight with the demons he brought home, J.P's life began to spiral downward in a few short years. Unable to hold onto a job, he became an embarrassment and, at times, a burden for his family. One could blame his troubles solely on alcoholism, but it is not that simple. War never is.

When Harold Nunnally, J.P.'s son, shared his father's letters with me I was fascinated by their clarity and honesty. J.P. had a gift for telling the truth and no matter how indelicate or embarrassing the acts in his recollections were he readily revealed them. In his correspondence J.P. is frank and painfully honest in exposing his fears, which explain his dependence upon alcohol.

Importantly, J.P. provides insight into his failure to build a civilian life. And even more so, no matter how difficult it had been to live, J.P.'s life ended with bittersweet success when he wrote his illuminating letters to his son. J.P.'s letters are timeless in the lesson they share about the cost of war. It is a message that is particularly relevant today.

When Harold shared these letters with me I was intrigued. When he told me that as an adult he could barely remember spending even a dozen hours in the company of his father I was compelled to tell the poignant story of this particular *Sailor Man*.

James "J.P." Nunnally at about the time of his illegal enlistment in 1943.

CHAPTER ONE

A Lovable Southern Country Boy

"I LOVED HIM MORE THAN I LOVED MY MOTHER AND FATHER," she said with a heartfelt sigh that bridges time. "But, of course, everyone loved J.P."

I challenged her, asking with just enough skepticism to prompt her for more. "Come on. No one is loved that much."

Audrey Alarcon-Rivera (nee Nunnally) responds to my challenge with a slight graceful drawl that hints back to her native Alabama. Even after the passage of decades the love in Audrey's voice is intense and pure when she recalls what her brother was like before he went off to fight in World War Two. "He was such a nice, sweet person before he left us. J.P. was a gentle and loving boy. Every person in Talladega who knew J.P. loved him."

"Everyone?" I express an even higher level of skepticism.

"Oh, yes," she firmly answers.

I pause before continuing. The J.P. Nunnally I have come to know is nothing like what she described. Honest? Yes. Interesting? Very much so. But, lovable? I think not.

I press to learn more about her brother. I say, "Tell me about him."

She laughs and tells me, "We called him Speedy because he was as slow as molasses in the winter. J.P. sang and was very musically inclined. He played the guitar and later, also the piano, to accompany his singing. It added to his popularity."

"What else do you remember about him before he went to war?" I asked. "Tell me why he was so loved."

"He was a caring person," Audrey explains. "J.P. was very caring, musical, and attractive—quite a combination. J.P. looked as good as he was kind. He was tall, six feet plus, with jet black hair and violet blue eyes. I idolized him."

To broaden the subject I asked, "What about your family? Tell me something about them."

"We were not originally from Talladega. Pell City, about twenty miles northwest, is where our family comes from. That was where J.P. was born in December 1926. He was the eldest of four boys and me. I'm the youngest and was born in 1936. When we were in Pell City we lived near the Cogswell crossroad. Back then, in the 1920s, '30s and '40s, the area was very rural. We were country folk."

"If he was born in 1926 that means he was only sixteen when he joined the Navy," I said. "The minimum legal age was seventeen, which means he enlisted illegally."

"Yes, that is correct," she said plainly. The family trait of being honest and direct is apparent.

I asked, "Do you have any idea how he skirted the rules?"

"No, I was very young. I had no idea about how he got around the age limit. I recall that my mother was against his enlisting, and I guess J.P. just lied about his age to get in."

"What else do you remember?'

"I just knew that J.P. couldn't wait and he quit school to go to war. He was a good student, but he got caught up in the enthusiasm to enlist and did not graduate high school. His childhood friend, Billy Black, joined the Navy with him very early in 1943. All he could do was talk about joining the Navy. It meant the world to him. J.P. was always looking at the Navy posters and reading the pamphlets that seemed to be with him all the time back then."

"Did he know anyone who was already in the Navy?"

"He may have, but I don't recall. What I do remember very clearly is that J.P. just wanted to be in the Navy more than anything in the world. I believe the decision was all his own."

"What was it like when he came home?" I asked.

"He was so very different—no longer the most kind-hearted person you'd ever meet."

Her voice trails off. I wait. She continues, "J.P. couldn't stand the noises at the mill where he worked. He had two nervous break downs. They put him in the VA hospital and gave him shock treatments."

She goes silent again.

And again, I wait.

Finally, the sister who adored him so much describes the J.P. who came home. "After the war, my brother was never the same. He was just never the same."

The full front cover of the document which helped lure J.P. into illegally enlisting.

CHAPTER TWO

"This Is Your War!"

T HE YEAR 1943 WAS A TIME BEFORE TELEVISION, cable, wi-fi, cellphones, and the Internet. During that era many of society's concepts, ideas, and ideals were routinely communicated by word of mouth, the radio, movie house newsreels, and various print formats. Newspapers, magazines, and popular periodicals such as *Time, Look, Life,* and the *Saturday Evening Post* were familiar items in most homes. Air time on the radio was filled predominately by entertainment and the medium's news content, as well as movie house newsreels, was better suited as a vehicle for the delivery of exciting and interesting facts rather than in-depth analysis. Consequently, in the early 1940s, many people's opinions were heavily influenced by their reading materials.

For young men like J.P. and his friend Billy knowledge of naval service was attained primarily through materials which came from the Navy itself in the form of recruiting pamphlets. One such offering was the highly popular "Men Make The Navy... The Navy Makes Men," which expertly combined the themes of patriotism, romance of the sea, and masculine camaraderie with economic opportunity and concrete benefits.

From the first look it is easy to image the appeal this sort of publication had on impressionable American teenagers. It boldly declares that the war is theirs, making participation a personal challenge that must be decisively and immediately addressed.

From the poster:

THIS IS YOUR WAR

Never in all history has the call for defenders of freedom been so urgent as at this moment.

Brave men are needed—stout-hearted men—men who would rather fight to stay free than live to be slaves.

If that's the way you feel about it, your place right now is with the Navy—your Navy—in America's first line of attack—shoulder to shoulder with the red-blooded men of action who are determined to defeat the Axis, who are not only remembering Pearl Harbor—but are doing something about it.

It's your war—as well as theirs. And the Navy needs your help to win it. All the warships, all the fighting planes America can produce, count for nothing without the men to man them. Skilled men who know their jobs. Fighting men who want action. Patriots who love their country—and serve it as true Americans should.

TO EVERY MAN WHO WANTS TO SERVE HIS COUNTRY

You have an important decision to make.

Today, every true American is asking himself one question. It comes from the heart: "How can I help my country most?"

Many of your friends have already answered your country's call to service. More will be going. You, too, are ready, eager to do your part. But you want to serve, and rightly so, where America needs you most—where you can do the most for your country, and for yourself.

Clearly, the Navy was relying on patriotism as the prime motivator for enlistees. However, there were additional points to be made. Facing the reality of the draft was an important inducement for eligible men to consider. The notion that it is better to select a branch of service (i.e., the Navy) than to be assigned to the Army or Marines was married to the idea that time was running out.

Again, from the poster:

CHOOSE NOW WHILE YOU CAN.
Make your decision carefully. But make it while you still have time. Choose a service that will give you action, thrills, adventure, travel. A service where you'll live a rugged, healthy, outdoor life that will build you up physically. A service that will make you an expert at a skilled trade, fit you to do a better fighting job now, fit you to land a better peacetime job later on.

Take a step you will be proud of all your life—volunteer now for the United States Navy.

You must act quickly.

Many men who have delayed too long in volunteering for the Navy now regret it. Don't wait till it's too late. Choose your service while you are still free to do so. Remember, even though you have received your orders to report for induction under Selective Service, you may still volunteer for the Navy. You can do so right up to the actual moment of your induction.

This was an important argument. In 1943 the age for registering for compulsory service was eighteen with selection coming soon thereafter. Like all physically able young men J.P. could expect to be drafted within a short period following his eighteenth birthday, or graduation from high school. Choice and urgency were certainly points that resonated with J.P.; so much so, in fact, that he enlisted illegally at the age of sixteen.

Also, his ego must have been in the mix. The Navy made no bones about its view that it was the preferred branch of the military and it boldly stated so:

> There are no finer men in all the world than those who serve in the United States Navy.
>
> As our Navy is great—so are its men. Red-blooded Americans who have got what it takes to fight for their country. Men who are physically fit, mentally alert. Men of action, men of responsibility. Men who live up to the glorious tradition of courage and heroism that has made the U. S. Navy the finest in the world.

Layered heavily on top of the call for patriot duty the Navy skillfully presented its economic benefits. All the offerings of Navy life—bed, board, pay, and health care benefits—were explained in detail. Pragmatic options for learning a trade and obtaining an education were listed, with the ultimate bait of attending the Naval Academy being mentioned without any specifics on the possibility. Finally, the allure of travel was included for added spice.

The pamphlet was an impressive marketing tool, and if J.P. had any doubt in the merit of his decision, it most probably melted before the Navy's powerful presentation of the ultimate appeal to a young man's ego: "You, Too Can Write Your Name In Your Country's History."

Considering the circumstances of the times, the potency of the argument, and its powerful presentation, how could a patriotic citizen not enthusiastically respond to the call to defend his country?

Early in 1943, James Preston Nunnally, a sixteen-year-old boy, illegally enlisted in the U.S. Navy with the dream of becoming the type of Sailor Man depicted on the pamphlet.

In his own words, here is J.P.'s story....

CHAPTER THREE

The War According to J.P.

Harold,
I will try through a series of letters to give you a little
run down on WWII...

W ITH THESE WORDS J.P. NUNNALLY BEGAN a lengthy correspondence with Harold, his estranged son. His remarkably candid account came in response to Harold simply asking his alienated father, "What happened?"

Then in his forties, Harold wanted to know more about the absentee father that had allowed him to be raised by relatives. Harold explained that he asked the question of his father because, "I had a great deal of anger and hostility toward the situation and him. Over time I mellowed out, but I just wanted to know why he was the way he was." According to his son, J.P. was the man "who was seldom there" and "was incapable of functioning in this world."

As with other seemingly uncomplicated questions, Harold's query is a request that can only be satisfied through a lengthy and complex explanation, and J.P. proved to be up to the task. His response was to provide an in-depth answer through the production of hundreds of pages of correspondence.

Also contained within the initial query are other questions, such as: "What did you feel?" "What did you see?" "Were you scared?" and, "How and when did alcohol become the curse and not the cure?"

Without hesitation, in a direct and open manner, J.P. attempted to answer all for Harold. In plain language he recounts his service in the Pacific Theater of World War Two and through his straightforward approach sheds light and insight on a life that was forever transformed by the trauma of war. Following a self-deprecating appraisal of his ability as a narrator J.P does not hold back in describing the horrible aspects of his wartime experience.

I can't do much to convey to you such things as the stench of death, the oily, greasy, dirty tore up shell-mutilated bodies and dead men. I can't convey to you the fear on both my and other's facial features until their expressions are nothing but frozen fear and dread and our faces look like they came out of a damned deep freeze.

J.P. maintains his blunt approach and proceeds to describe the enormity of facing death while continuing to perform your duty, a daunting task for anyone, certainly more so for one so young.

How can I explain to you how it feels to resign your soul to God and eternity and your body to a gallon of embalming fluid, or the goddamn rat that keeps gnawing at your intestines. and yet there is a sanity in this goddamn insane operation. You, a man, a sailor, or soldier, you have work to do and come hell, high water, death, destruction, life or death, you keep on doing, shooting, shitting, or working, hollering, groaning, praying, cussing. You keep on doing your job like a goddamn man is supposed to do and after you wonder how in hell you and others were able to do so.

Surprisingly, relief came to J.P. in the form of the routine, and at times the drudgery, of his wartime service. It was a topic not covered in the recruiting pamphlets that absorbed young J.P.'s attention. In his looking back, J.P. had no illusions about the romance and adventure of military service.

Most of the time it's only work, work, work—making preparations, doing without rest and sleep—planning—training—dull boring work . Most of war is work, planning, education. It is mostly a dull goddamn absolute nothing. Most of the time you spend wishing you were far far away somewhere else.

SAILOR MAN

CHAPTER FOUR

Doing One's Duty

Although J.P's letters contain clear and specific remembrances of his commendable and colorful wartime experiences, they are at times surprisingly short on some vital details. For example, the date of his enlistment, boot camp, specialty training, and his initial assignment in Hawaii are barely described, if mentioned at all. Even his illegal under-aged enlistment goes unmentioned.

However, the absence of those items is not crucial to telling his story. For J.P., "the war" only meant the time he served aboard the USS *Fuller*. As a reader of recruiting pamphlets, J.P. got what he wished for and the exuberant and patriotic teenager landed duty aboard a ship that earned fame as the "Queen of Attack Transports."

He writes:

> *Harold,*
> *Perhaps before we go farther we should take time to learn something about our operations and everyday*

The USS *Fuller,* legendary *Queen of Attack Transports,* earned nine battle stars in the Pacific Theater after performing admirably in the North Atlantic and Caribbean.

life aboard the USS Fuller, APA-7, (code name in radio transmissions as Del Rio-7). First of all, we were not a warship (in the classic sense, like a battleship or destroyer) and we could operate better if we ran into no trouble instead of attacking elements of the Jap war machine. The ship was crewed by 590 men and officers. We could carry anywhere from 1,600 to 2,000 passengers, Marines, Army, CB's, and so forth.

We were about 550 feet long and 60 feet at the beam. We were armed with four 3 inch pieces of navy *artillery. At one time we had a 5 inch gun which is as big as the main batteries of a Fletcher Class destroyer. Every time the gun was fired it put the laundry underneath the gun out of commission. Finally, it was removed and a twin 40mm was installed in its place.*

When I was aboard the ship, we were armed with four 3" guns on two main batteries, both forward and aft, near the stern of the ship. We also had nine 20mm AA (anti-aircraft) and two twin 40mm AA added to this when we had ten 50 cal MGs (machine guns) and 38 light 30 cal MGs, a pretty good AA gun.

We spent many days and nights going from island to island, picking up troops, supplies and transporting them around from place to place in the Pacific, south, central, and southwest and sometimes in Asian waters of the Pacific.

We greased machinery, painted, and worked on boats. Also, there was gun practice and general quarters (battle stations) just before daylight in the mornings and just before dark in the evenings.

We carried troops and supplies and took them into beaches on D-day where the Jap was generally ready with their field artillery to try to blow us out of the water when we carried the troops in boats and assorted landing craft. We had quite a few air raids which done some damage to the larger ships. Generally speaking, except for rare occasions, the Jap aircraft didn't waste their time attacking landing craft.

Most of our time was spent far out to sea. There are vast stretches of ocean far away from military

*installations, shipping routes that can hide a dozen
navies in them, out of range of aircraft and hidden
by the vastness of the open sea. There, we were about
as safe from Jap attack as we could be.*

J.P. constantly played down the value of his service by saying
he was not aboard a "warship." That was not how Admiral
William F. "Bull" Halsey, Commander of the South Pacific, saw
it. In a letter to his command Halsey gives credit to his "non-
combatant" sailors, he wrote: "Your resourcefulness, tireless
ingenuity, cooperation and indomitable fighting spirit form a
battle pattern that will everywhere be an inspiration, and a great
measure of the credit for the sky blazing, sea sweeping, jungle
smashing of the combat forces goes to the construction gangs
and service organizations that bulldozed bases out of the jungle
and brought up the beans and bullets and supplies."

Such exemplary service was commonplace aboard J.P.'s
home, the USS *Fuller*. Its reputation was excellent and widely
known. The *Fuller* was the perfect place for J.P. to become the
Sailor Man depicted in the recruiting literature.

CHAPTER FIVE

"His" Ship

I N A REVEALING AND ILLUMINATING ARTICLE ABOUT THE USS *Fuller*, Marine Corps Combat Correspondent Staff Sergeant Maurice E. Moran filed this report on the ship that would be J.P's home for more than two and a half years. Moran's in-theater report appeared in several wartime publications:

(Dateline unknown, aboard a U.S. Navy Transport in the South Pacific)

Combat planes dip their wings in salute as they pass this ship because they recognize her as a queen with a glorious pedigree. She's ploughed through these waters so long that pilots regard her as a "landmark." Although old as ships go, she has played a dramatic part in America's war on the oceanic fronts.

Commissioned in 1919 as a cargo-passenger vessel, this transport was re-commissioned as a U.S. navy vessel in 1941. Since then she has rolled up an unbelievable record of "firsts in war."

She was in the convoy which transported U.S. Marines to Iceland, the first American troops to land on foreign soil in this global war. When the Japs' sneak punch forced America into the conflict, she helped transport the First American Expeditionary Force to the British Isles. On her return trip she served as a mercy ship, bringing hundreds of bomb-beleaguered British men, women, and children to haven in the United States.

Then she sailed into the Pacific.

Out here she became one of the first transports to land U.S. Marines at Guadalcanal. Her tough hide endured a rain of Jap bombs. On her bridge deck are emblazoned four tiny Jap flags, symbols of torpedo bombers who tried to get to her and fell before the marksmanship of her crew.

Since the first thrust at the Solomons, the *Queen* has been engaged in a perilous shuttle game, transporting troops and supplies to the area's hot spots and bringing out the wounded, sick and prisoners. She has had several close squeaks.

Several times she brought supplies to the Solomon forces on a hit-and-run basis, unloading until the bombs got too hot and then running out of the harbor until the raiders disappeared. Once when the Marines' supplies were virtually non-existent, the Old Lady saved the day by rushing in an overload of dry stores. Every inch of available space was used for food, including holds normally used for troops.

A ship bearing such distinction could be manned only by a gallant crew. Its first skipper, Captain Paul S. Theiss, USN, of Indiana, Pennsylvania, won the Navy Cross for his handling of the vessel in the Solomons. According to William E.V. Stewart, Boatswain's Mate First Class, USN, of Seattle, with the ship in all her adventures, Captain Theiss is "the fightingest man I ever saw—and our new old man is just like him."

Although J.P.'s ship was officially named USS *Fuller*, during the years of World War II, she was also known by additional names and designations: AP-14, APA-7, the *Queen*, and the *Old Girl* are just a few. To the battle-hardened marines and soldiers of the South Pacific she was *That Glorious Lady* and *The Only Ship in the Navy*. To her original commissioning crew of

Chicago reservists activated early in 1941 she naturally was known as *The Gangster*. Its assumption of the role as the epitome of World War Two's attack transports is a tale of both predestination and circumstance.

Examining the records of its origins reveal that the *Fuller* may have always been meant to be the *Queen of Attack Transports*. Originally laid out in 1916 at Bethlehem Steel's Alameda shipyard as the SS *War Wave* to fill a purchase request by the British Admiralty as a troop transport, it was renamed the SS *Archer* following the April 1917 entrance of the United States into World War One. And, as the *Archer*, it briefly did transport troops.

After the war the *Archer* was acquired by the Baltimore Mail Steamship Company for renovation and conversion to civilian duty, and following renovations, including lengthening of its hull and repowering, the *Archer* reappeared in 1931 as the *City of Newport News*.

Between wars, the future-fabled ship waited to fulfill its destiny. In November 1940 the *City of Newport News* was re-acquired by the U.S. Navy and renamed USS *Fuller*. As a prototype for the new class of ships known as attack transports, the *Fuller's* performance in the Atlantic and Caribbean was impressive. However, it was merely a precursor for the lead role it would take in delivering troops to the very front of battle—on the beaches of the South Pacific—where it earned a record nine battle stars. Indeed, the attack transport known in street slang as *The Gangster* was meant to be a warship.

By the time J.P. joined its crew in 1943, the *Fuller* was well on its way to becoming a legend. Due to its standout performance in the Solomons, the *Fuller's* original Captain had moved up. Yet, Paul Theiss's Navy Cross was only one part of an impressive three-way career boosting honor for *The Gangster's* skipper; he also received promotion to the special war-time one-star rank of Commodore and assignment as Chief of Staff for the amphibious forces under the command of Rear Admiral Richmond K. (Kelly) Turner. As the past commanding officer of the *Fuller*, newly promoted Commodore Theiss knew firsthand what the fabled ship was capable of accomplishing and his good fortune meant that the *Fuller* was guaranteed to continue being in the forefront of the Navy's combat efforts in the Southern Pacific Theater.

Duty in the North Atlantic, two battle stars for service at Guadalcanal, and standout performance in the Solomons were just the beginning of the *Fuller's* rise to prominence and recognition as the *Queen of Attack Transports*. Seven additional battle stars were in its future, and J.P. would be there to earn all of them.

CHAPTER SIX

New Ships for a New Kind of War

T HE U.S. NAVY'S PACIFIC STRATEGY, WHICH BECAME known as "island hopping," was dependent upon the deployment of a new type of vessel—the attack transport. Island hopping was a series of invasions aimed at bypassing highly fortified Japanese positions with the intent of leapfrogging from one island to another on a path toward the Japanese homeland. The success of the strategy was dependent upon blockading the Japanese within their key bases and then using attack transports to deliver allied troops to key islands on the way toward Japan. Attack transports were fundamental to the strategy's success.

Landings on island beaches, or amphibious assaults, required that troops be delivered in small boats from base ships which sat close offshore to targeted areas. The delivery of troops was accomplished by landing craft, usually LCVPs (landing craft, personnel) also known as Higgins boats, a thirty-six foot long shallow-draft landing craft. Troops generally entered the LCVP by climbing down cargo nets from the side of the ships; they disembarked at the beach by exiting down the boat's front-drop bow ramp.

Attack transports like the *Fuller* were expected to support and deliver up to a battalion of combat troops to a hostile beachhead utilizing LCVPs. After landing troops, an attack transport remained near the beachhead (at the front) to conduct support activities. From an anchored position as many as 1,500 troops and equipment were delivered to beaches and supported with food, medical supplies, ammunition and evacuation by using the LCVPs and other craft.

When shipboard stores were depleted the attack transports returned to rear area bases for resupply and shuttle service back to the beachheads. The to and fro trips for supplies and reinforcements were often in perilous conditions as these ships were high priority targets.

In late 1942 the Navy recognized that the type of duty performed by attack transports required a new designation, and early in 1943, to clearly describe these frontline amphibious service ships and their capabilities, they received a new designation—APA.

More often than not, accounts of war focus upon combat units at the front lines and war ships such as carriers, battleships, submarines, and destroyers. Regrettably, the heroic actions of other personnel under fire are often overlooked. Long after submarine warfare and air power has forever relocated the edge of the battlefield, logistic and support units are still seen as non-combatants. The battle tested attack transports of the Amphibious Force were just that—battle tested.

During the war APAs were often targets of torpedoes, bombs, and kamikazes. Six APAs were lost in combat, and of the thirteen ships in the *Fuller's* division only four were not sunk or badly damaged during the war. When J.P. joined its crew in 1943 the *Fuller* had already received its new designation as an

APA—Number 7. Its mission was to land troops on hostile beaches and support them through the most dangerous early days of combat. When describing his assignment J.P. wrongly considered himself not to have served aboard a "warship." Soon after joining the *Fuller* he would experience what being aboard an APA really meant.

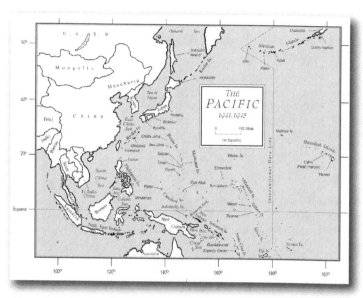

Map of the Pacific Theatre of Operations, 1941-1945.

CHAPTER SEVEN

The Day the
Bombs Dropped

Harold,

*I don't know how many air raids I have been in,
probably more than a hundred. But a large part of
the time the Japanese simply did not send enough
planes to do a whole lot of damage.*

O N NOVEMBER 8, 1943 THE JAPANESE SENT more than enough
planes. The overall target was the Marine landing on the
island of Bougainville at Empress Augusta Bay. In particular,
the Japanese sent a deadly dive bomber formation which
targeted the *Fuller*.

Bougainville was the largest of the Solomon Islands and had
been a Japanese stronghold for almost two years. Their retreat
from Guadalcanal in early 1943 made it all the more important
for them to hold it. If the Japanese lost Bougainville, they would
lose their naval base at Rabaul and be forced to retreat 800
miles north to Truk. Therefore, the Japanese were prepared to
defend Bougainville and their air attacks were intense.

The *Fuller's* wartime record has been superbly chronicled by crewmember Albert C. Allen, who later became a noted journalist for Louisville's *Courier-Journal*. Allen's account is semi-official, as he had access to the ship's log and action reports, and has been recognized as an authoritative record of the *Fuller's* exploits.

From that account:

We arrived at Empress Augusta Bay on the morning of November 8th and began unloading immediately. There was no opposition until about noon, at which time we received warning of a strong force of "Bogies" approaching from the northward. Apparently a part of this force was broken up by the Combat Air Patrol, since only about twenty of them got through. The transports got underway immediately, forming to repel attack. It was not long in developing.

The screen was first to open fire on a group of torpedo planes attempting to break into the formation. These were repelled. At nearly the same time, dive bombers began to pour out of the clouds like rain drops. Seven peeled off and made for the Fuller, as the transports opened fire. We happened to be the last ship in column, and as such were a most attractive target.

One of the raiders was caught by a 3" burst and exploded before his dive had fairly begun. The other six, however, did their best to make up for the loss of their comrade. Four bombs burst in a close pattern around the ship's bow. The last of these was a near miss which perforated the side with shrapnel holes, killing one man and wounding several others. The bomber which laid his egg succumbed to a concentrated burst of fire from the 20mms and crashed in flames on the starboard side.

The other two made for the after part of the ship. The first bomb, badly aimed, landed some distance in the wake of the ship. The final bomb, however, was far more destructive than the concentrated fury of the preceding

Empress Augusta Bay, December 8, 1943. Troops embarking from an APA the day J.P. first saw combat.

six combined. It hit number four 3″ gun, ricocheted through the after battery splinter shield, and went sailing down the ladder to the crew's compartment, where it exploded halfway to its destination.

It is lucky for the ship that the bomb ricocheted; otherwise it would have exploded in the after magazine, causing an explosion from which the ship could not possibly have survived.

As J.P. recounts the day's events for Harold:

*We were hit off the coast of Bougainville in the
Solomon Islands not far from Guadalcanal. Killed 13
and wounded 27. The 550 lb. bomb hit our port 3"
anti-aircraft gun, bent the barrel into an S shape,
then went through three steel decks and exploded
near the magazine for the after gun.*

More from the ship's account:

At the end of the attack, the formation returned to the
transport area, and resumed debarkation of troops and
unloading. As the day drew to a close, the reports of
readiness to get underway began to go to the flag, and
lo, the name of the *Fuller* led all the rest! Our damage
control parties had done their work with amazing
competence and speed, while the deck divisions
continued unloading as before, with all hands trying to
compensate for the loss of their shipmates by doing more
than their share.

On that day combat and death became a reality for the then
sixteen year old. The legendary ship that he was fortunate to be
part of had downed three dive bombers, and still completed
its mission while it was bombed and set afire.

In his letter to Harold, perhaps still compensating for his
loss, J.P. avoids highlighting his role as a firefighter in the
damage control party where there is a high probability that
his duties included the extraction of the dead and dying from
the bomb site. Instead, he briefly and matter-of-factly states:

The men were buried at sea.

On November 8, 1943, J.P. was still six weeks from his seventeenth birthday. One can only wonder how this experience affected him, as a teenager in real and not imagined combat; we cannot specifically know without a contemporary account. However, years later as he recounted his service to his son, J.P.'s approach and tone in his letters take a dramatic turn. From this point on J.P. becomes more open about his use and abuse of numbing substances, primarily alcohol.

For example, after a meticulous and impressive description of military equipment and armaments on both aircraft and vessels (torpedo planes, observation planes, three types of aircraft carriers, battleships, heavy and light cruisers, destroyers, destroyer escorts, LSTs, LCIs, LTVs, LCVPs, and LCMs) J.P. tells the following tale about illicit shipboard alcohol.

He shares:

It (the LCM) had two 230 horse power diesel engines, a small engine room below the weather deck where you could dry clothes or heat up canned "C" rations on one of the engine's manifolds, store lots of odds and ends and hide a couple of gallons of apple jack made from apple juice or raisin jack made from raisins, sugar, yeast and water.

My engineer, a fellow named Merietta, had vast talent when it came to stealing everything that wasn't tied down or welded to the steel deck—canned hams, candy, Army rations, cigarettes, and coffee. In short, all of the available things to steal lying around (which was plenty). I wouldn't go as far as to describe him as a first-rate thief, Hell that was far too mild a term for him and his vast talents. A master craftsman at thievery, perhaps, but not an ordinary common thief.

He was also a loyal shipmate and a good friend, albeit a contrary one at times. He could turn out some reasonable extra fine raisin jack, which on one occasion got him to setting in a deck chair carrying on a conversation with the big beautiful tropical moon. I guess I loved that man even if he was two ranks above me. Still, I was Boat Commander, or the Coxswain, an operator and navigator, so that made him subordinate to me. I gave the orders and he took fine care of his engines, kept us in supplies from his diplomatic thievery, and with the help of his mechanical ability and his good raisin jack we got along fine.

CHAPTER EIGHT

Saipan—June 1944

A BOUT THE TIME WHEN HIS CLASSMATES AT HOME were graduating Pell City High School in Alabama, J.P. was in the South Pacific facing much more than a cap and gown ceremony. Already battle tested, and a witness to combat deaths, seventeen year old J.P. shuttled troops in and out of the Pacific's bloodiest battle to date, at Saipan. His memory of that violent event was remarkably clear, however it will not remain so for subsequent and even more violent military actions.

About Saipan he wrote:

Harold,

It was June. Spring and early summer were in the air. It was a time that devastation, death, and hardship was to come to the civilians and troops of the Imperial Japanese Navy, Marines, and Army of a most esteemed and honorable general whose name [Lt. Gen. Yoshitsugu Saito] I forgot. Against him was arrayed the considerable military might of the U.S.A.

Warships dotted the area, battleships, both light and heavy cruisers, destroyers and numerous lighter

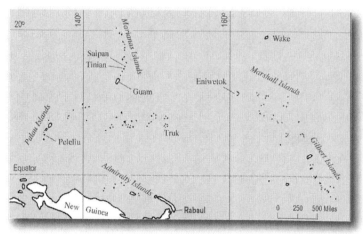

Map of Saipan's location in the South Pacific.

vessels, including D.E.s (WWI destroyers or destroyer escorts). Many vessels, battleships, cruisers, and D.D.s (destroyers) were firing inland, some into the hills on the island, others seemed to be firing on Garapan, the capitol of the island, where a big sugar mill was built by civilians and Japanese workers imported to the island from the Nippon Empire.

I was a young sailor on the USS Fuller, named after an obscure admiral in the U.S. Navy. We were an APA (Amphibious Personnel-Assault)—a troop transport caring assault units of the U.S. Marine Divisions 2 and 4, and some elements of the 5th.

J.P. describes with respect the men he would ferry to the battlefield. Men who were the marine equivalent of the sailors described in the recruiting pamphlets. (The ship's namesake,

B. H. Fuller, Naval Academy Class of 1889, had been a Marine Major General and Commandant of the Marine Corps.)

Trained in amphibious warfare they were crack elite assault forces capable of taking on ten times their number of the best trained army of the world. They were solemn men, no shit, no brag, no bad asses, no liars among them. Just men who were good at their jobs of bringing death, suffering, destruction, and defeat to an enemy they did not hate but were determined to beat the hell out of and make believers out of the sons of bitches. I had the same thought as the other men, by god we had come to kick their asses and come hell or a rip tide we meant it if it was in our power to do just that.

Flame throwers were tested aboard ship, B.A.R.s (Browning Automatic Rifles), rifles, carbines, were test fired into the water. Officers made speeches over the P.A. system to their troops, company commanders checked their men and equipment. They ate in the crew's mess closest to their men, they treated their troops with loving care, trying to be father and comrade to the men. I had a lot of respect for Captains or C.O.s they treated their men like their own brothers.

Finally, when the firing stopped, we were ready to invade the island. Boats of all kinds were loaded with troops who climbed over the ship's side down cargo nets into the boats. Men had machine gun belts crisscrossed over their shoulders. Mortar crews carried 60mm and 81mm mortars. One man carried the tube or barrel and another carried the breast plate which was the mount. Two men carried satchels of ammo for that ordnance piece. Four men were in a mortar crew, each man was issued three frag grenades.

A Browning Automatic Rifleman carried lots of pounds of ammo, plus a 22 lb. auto rifle. All of the men's skin was yellow as hell from taking Atabrine an antimalarial drug which was a substitute for quinine.

Boats and "ducks" of all kinds such as LCMs, LCVPs , and LVTs were in the water everywhere loaded with ammo, rations, water, and gasoline going around in tight circles waiting for H hour. It was D-day at Saipan and the Imperial Japanese forces were waiting to open up with their devastating artillery when the boats came into range of the beach which were mined and (covered) by machine gun emplacements.

Ducks carried troops, cargo, and two 50 cal. machine guns and they and their amphibious naval personnel would take care of many machine gun emplacements on the sandy beaches such as Blue Beach, Red Beach, White Beach, Black Beach I and II and III, Purple Beach and so forth. Planes, Navy Hellcats, Corsairs, and others were over the island strafing AA emplacements of the Imperial Japanese forces.

Well, the landing craft went ashore to run into artillery fire. It took its toll of boats, cargo, and troops. If a shell hit into a boat loaded with drums of gasoline, ammo, or into diesel fuel tanks the whole goddam thing turned into a fireball which nothing escapes alive. I saw several such occurrences. All of this was dangerous work for everyone involved. The gods of death, hell, and destruction must have had a heyday on D-day at Saipan. But the worst was yet to come from their emissaries—the green blow flies feasting off of almost 2,000 bodies floating in the water. Seems

Saipan's barrier reef and lagoon created an arduous landing site where J.P. worked to the point of delerium.

like about 1,500 civilians decided to end their lives by jumping off a cliff into the rocks and water along with some Jap soldiers to keep from getting captured. Amen.

Although only seventeen, J.P. must have been a very capable sailor. The *Fuller's* compliment of Higgins boats numbered only about two dozen. To be a coxswain during an invasion, especially at Saipan, was not an insignificant assignment.

J.P. shared how gruesome and grueling the duty could be as a crewman aboard one of the landing craft:

One time after an unbelievable shelling, when I had twelve wounded men in my boat, which was badly damaged, I went into a state of mental shock. I thought maybe I was dead, "killed by shellfire and back to earth in spirit form." I didn't know for sure whether I was dead or not, so being the wise ass I was I spoke to my crew, figuring if I was still alive and could hear them answer me, I was still alive. I spoke to my engineer and he answered me, then the awful goddam truth hit me, I could hear them because we were all dead, the whole damn bunch of us, and we were just back to earth in spirit form. It was about three days before I realized that, hell, we were still alive and not back to earth in spirit form. I was in shock.

Years later (and still in denial?), J.P. adds:

Ha Ha! Everything O.K. War is hell.

In retrospect he comments further upon Saipan, where at least 30,000 Japanese troops perished, and more than 13,000 Americans were casualties:

I suppose war is O.K. to those who read about it, but my skinny ass kept asking one question, "Nunnally, you crazy son of a bitch. What are you doing in this goddam crazy lash up?" Yeah, I wish I was far far away, anywhere but here, ha ha. Amen.

J.P.'s wish was not fulfilled. He would only be going as far as Tinian—for another invasion.

CHAPTER NINE

Doing It Again
at Tinian

N OT MENTIONED BY J.P. WAS THE *FULLER'S* SPECIAL ROLE in the
Saipan invasion. Most probably tapped by Commodore
Theiss for special duty, the *Fuller* participated in a faux invasion
to deceive the Japanese defenders into fruitless action on the
wrong beach.

From the ship's account:

We arrived off Saipan in the early morning of June
fifteenth. Standing into transport area our division formed
with Transport Division 10 and other units, a demonstration
group 52.9 under Captain G.D. Morrison, to make a feint
at Beaches Black 1 and 2, and Scarlett 1 and 2. We slowed,
lowered boats, and dispatched landing craft towards the
beach. Meanwhile the main force had arrived off the
southern end of the island, and were doing the same. They,
however, were not faking. The purpose of our feint was to
draw some of the opposition from the main landing beaches
to the northern end of the island. The measure of its success
may be judged by a broadcast from Radio Tokyo, to the
effect that a large landing force had been repulsed by
Saipan's "heroic defenders" at Garapan [on Saipan's
northern tip].

Nothing succeeds like success, and the same tactics were applied on the southern end of neighboring Tinian.

Again, from the ship's account:

> In view of our previous success in the line of feinting, our division was ordered to repeat the tactics of the Saipan invasion.
>
> Meanwhile, the main landing was in progress on the northern end of the island. The Japs had been pulled so far out of position by our feint on the southern end of the island that all they could bring to bear on the narrow, exposed, main landing were small caliber guns and a few mortars. The beachhead there was made with few casualties. Our feint successful, we recalled our boats, hoisted them aboard, and joined the main force. In due time, we sent our troops ashore and unloaded our cargo.

J.P. remembered Tinian well, as it was a relatively peaceful engagement.

He recounts:

Harold,

We were to make a fake landing with empty boats and assorted landing craft on the beaches of one side of the island while the real landings, with assault forces (marines) made the real landing on the other side. Our purpose was to draw Japanese forces and equipment such as field artillery to the hills closest around the fake landing sites. We succeeded in doing so. There were approximately 9,000 enemy troops on the island.

I had attended lectures, briefings, and examined top secret War Department documents, so I know roughly what Jap strength and equipment, fortifications, beaches defenses the Jap had and so on. We were to go in an empty landing craft (with crew only) to 3,000 yards of the beach to draw fire and tie up the whole damn Jap force if we could. We succeeded beyond our wildest dreams. Against 9,000 Japanese only 159 marines were killed in the campaign.

I was given a bag of square wood plugs and a hammer to drive into shrapnel holes in the boat. Luckily, there were no holes made in the boat. Damage and casualties were light, although at a few hundred yards I saw a couple of boats get hit in the fuel tanks and turned into fireballs. Nobody lived through that hell's furnace I'm sure.

As we went into the beach at least a hundred pieces of artillery up in the hills were flashing when they fired shells, were chewing up the beaches, and some were hitting in our vicinity although we turned back at 3,000 yards. It was dark, just before dawn, the reason we could see the flashes from the artillery. All in all it was a howling success, the Jap was fooled completely. None of our ships were firing on the Jap artillery as we went in. That alone should have made the Jap suspicious, but by then it was far too late for the Jap to rectify his mistake. The real landing was almost unopposed and it too was a howling success.

Next day we unloaded troops, tanks, artillery, rations, ammo, water, gasoline, trucks, and half-tracks at the original landing site. We met no enemy fire. The marines had advanced inland 2-3 miles and set fire to numerous ammo and fuel dumps as well as abandoned Jap equipment.

There was very little air traffic over the island, no Jap planes appeared, and the whole operation went smoothly as possible. It was a beautiful picture story book operation from all standpoints from beginning to end. Less than thirty days were needed to secure the area although mopping up operations continued for some time. As usual, very few prisoners were taken.

We received about forty prisoners a few days later. Some of them were as old as 50 or 60 years old, some young; quite a few were slightly wounded. All were courteous and well behaved, although most were a little sullen, quiet, and subdued. We took them to Eniwetok in the Marshall Islands for imprisonment. No incidents occurred on the trip. We fed them very good, did not mistreat them in any way, treated them medically, gave them clothes, underwear, candy, and cigarettes. For sake of security we guarded them with '03 rifles and Thompson submachine guns. End of story, a beautiful operation, the best I ever saw.

The beauty and ease of the Tinian feint and invasion would disappear entirely in the Palau Islands, where J.P. participated in the assault and capture of Peleliu, perhaps the hardest fought and most difficult engagement for any U.S. forces engaged anywhere in World War Two.

CHAPTER TEN

Peleliu—Hell on Earth

T HE NATIONAL MUSEUM OF THE MARINE CORPS calls the campaign on Peleliu, "the bitterest battle of the war," and during September to December 1944 the aptly named *Operation Stalemate II* was truly the location where hell resided on earth. In some opinions, what has become the "Forgotten Battle of the Pacific War" was indeed America's toughest in World War Two, perhaps its most difficult ever.

It was on Peleliu that the Japanese perfected their tactics to support and defend the newly created "Absolute National Defense Zone." Peleliu was an important position on the zone's perimeter and it was to be held at all costs. The Japanese military leadership vowed that Peleliu would not be taken.

In their defense of Peleliu, the Japanese would no longer seriously man and defend the landing beaches. After experiencing heavy aerial and naval bombardments, they chose to only lightly defend the beaches and instead withdraw to fortified positions inland. Also, suicidal banzai charges, such as the one containing almost 3,000 on Saipan, were abandoned in favor of well planned, small-scale night counter-attacks. The strategy was attrition—to bleed the invaders.

The hellish details of Peleliu will not be recounted here in detail. But the following statistics may describe the ferocity of the engagement: one in every three U.S. combatants became a casualty, and of the approximately 11,000 Japanese defenders, 10,695 were killed, with only 202 being captured. Added to the mix were torrid weather conditions: no breeze and temperatures at 105 degrees, with peaks of 115, and flies.

The most vivid description of the fight for Peleliu is in Eugene Sledge's *With the Old Breed: At Peleliu and Okinawa*. In this book Sledge writes, Peleliu was a "nether world of horror from which escape seemed less and less likely as casualties mounted and the fighting dragged on and on. Time had no meaning; life had no meaning. The fierce struggle made savages of us all." The men he served with on Peleliu, "suffered so much for their country. None came out unscathed. Many gave their lives, their health and some their sanity."

It is said that those experiencing trauma often remember everything or nothing at all. J.P.'s letter concerning Peleliu is his briefest recounting of any action in which he participated.

Harold,

I can't remember a whole lot about this one. Troop strength (Jap) unknown to me. Very dangerous campaign for boat crews. One reason, reefs surrounded these atolls and landing craft had to wait until high tide to go over the reefs. That high rough water caused all kinds of trouble, crews of craft got breached on high reefs and Jap mortars and artillery caused many casualties. Much M.G. fire hit troops and boat crews at the landing sites. Exact casualty rate of U.S. and Jap unknown, but

J.P. and pals aboard the USS *Fuller*. J.P. is center-rear wearing a white T-shirt.

very high for two small atolls. Costly campaign. Still aboard USS Fuller, *APA-7. No Jap aircraft or fleet activity to speak of. More later about the night the Japanese fleet bottled us up in Leyte Gulf and the biggest naval battle in history took place.*

Harold, take care. Write or I'll put an awful curse upon your puny pumpkin head ha ha.

Love to all,

J.P., the sailor man

His humorous, and somewhat awkward, closing serves as the setup for his telling postscript. More than forty years later, the experiences of Peleliu once again drove J.P. to the comfort he found in alcohol, a predictable response for someone experiencing post-traumatic stress disorder.

He writes further:

P.S. Harold, took the $20, and got four bottles of cheap wine. Got about drunk as you can tell by reading that drunk-ass letter I wrote. Forgive me.

In assessing J.P.'s condition it must be remembered that at Saipan he was shelled into delirium and by all standards Peleliu was worse. One must ask: What sort of hell did the still boyish sailor experience at Peleliu? The answer will never be known because J.P. cannot remember. Which is understandable as it is a common response to trauma. As also is his retreat into the numbing embrace of alcohol. J.P.'s memory loss is strong evidence that he was a victim of post-traumatic stress. His reliance on alcohol is further and very compelling proof of his damaged status.

CHAPTER ELEVEN

Post-Traumatic
Stress Disorder

D ANGER AND FEAR SO OFTEN GO HAND IN HAND. When confronted
with a disturbing experience the natural reaction of fear
triggers numerous split-second changes in the body to defend
against or avoid danger. Normally this is a built-in healthy
reaction meant to protect a person from harm. What is known
as Post Traumatic Stress Disorder is this "fight or flight" reaction
gone astray by unpredictable and uncontrollable memories and
production of severe anxiety, the symptoms of which can appear
immediately after the initial event or, sometimes, even years
later.

The condition has only been identified as post-traumatic
stress disorder, or PTSD, since 1980. Prior to then, in relation
to combat conditions, it was known by numerous names. Jacob
Mendez da Costa first studied it in regard to Civil War veterans
and his name was attached to it as Da Costa Syndrome, or
alternately "irritable heart" or "soldier's heart." The prevalence
of massed cannons and heavy artillery barrages in World War
One led to the name of shell shock, which then evolved between

the wars into post-concussion syndrome, combat stress reaction, combat fatigue, and finally, combat exhaustion.

Regardless of its name, the military's view of the condition has been for the most part unsympathetic, with the diagnosis often being attributed to character flaws, if not outright cowardice. During WWI at least one soldier was executed for refusing to return to combat duty after suffering acute shell shock. Non-physical ailments have always been viewed negatively by all military organizations. By contrast, in J.P.'s favorite pamphlet prospective U.S. Navy recruits were called upon to, "show they've got the stuff," in their pursuit of "the kind of action and adventure that thrills a he-man down to his toes!"

PTSD occurs after particularly terrifying ordeals, and the obvious fact is that the adrenalin filled horror of combat is the perfect breeding ground for its development. Often a survivor, or witness, particularly young ones, can be most affected by a traumatic event. Sleep disorders, sensitivity to sounds and vibrations, profound changes in thought, and hyper arousal are just a few of the ongoing problems victims of PTSD encounter. Also, in reliving their traumatic events or avoiding them alltogether, victims of PTSD often seek numbing substances, such as alcohol, to block out negative feelings and uncontrollable emotions.

As a crew member of an attack transport in the midst of the South Pacific's most horrendous fighting, it is understandable that J.P. would encounter the ingredients of PTSD. Also, being a non-high school graduate and under-aged at enlistment he possessed two of the key heightened indicators for developing the condition. Living through the Bougainville bombing of the *Fuller*, fighting the onboard fire, watching men die, and burying them at sea, these events are a lot for any teenager to experience.

Add to those experiences his Saipan and Peleliu combat duty and the only logical conclusion is that J.P. indeed did develop PTSD. His subsequent behavior and its reliance upon alcohol should remove any doubt as to the diagnosis.

SAILOR MAN

CHAPTER TWELVE

Just "Another Day at Work"

A NOTHER REASON J.P. MAY NOT HAVE BEEN ABLE to fully recall Peleliu is due to the *Fuller* being immediately involved in another invasion. In October of 1944, while fighting still continued on Peleliu, J.P.and his shipmates were tapped to participate in yet another operation. The assignment was the first of two landings in the Philippines.

J.P., only two months and two days away from his eighteenth birthday and already a seasoned veteran, dutifully delivered troops to the beach at Leyte Gulf. Then, he and his shipmates aboard the *Fuller* evaded the massive Japanese force bent on repulsing General MacArthur's return to the Philippines.

He writes:

Harold,

Leyte Island, in the Philippines. Considerable air activity in this campaign. (By the time the war was over at Okinawa, everyone agreed we had shot down ten and a half Jap planes. Although we only got credit for seven, plus knocking out a gun turret on a Jap cruiser dead in the water from torpedo hits.) This cruiser business happened at Guadalcanal before I signed aboard the Fuller.

On D-day we anchored 7 miles offshore and waited for H-hour. We were in the 15th wave going in. Troops were so damn scared when the artillery barrage began that they looked like their expressions were frozen. I guess maybe I looked that way, too. I never been in such hellacious shellfire in my life. The whole ocean was churning, and shrapnel was flying everywhere, whining like a swarm of hornets. Every piece of it sounded like it was coming straight at my head. I spent a lot of time trying to duck shrapnel (too slow).

We took a few hits, but very little damage, nobody hurt. Just before a monstrous shell hit among the troops on the beach I saw 3 big coconut palms uprooted by the big shell and blew them high into the air. They tumbled in slow motion until they fell to the ground. We unloaded our troops (disembarked them) unto the beach. No more shells hit the beach although I was worried that they would start again. Shells were still exploding off shore where later waves of landing craft were about to arrive.

We had to haul the casualties to medical facilities on ships. As the Army or Marine troops began loading wounded men machine gun fire began sawing up the sand within feet of the wounded and the men handling them. I instructed the troops to shift to the port side and manned the starboard 30 cal. light machine gun. I looked out to locate the source of the incoming m.g. fire about 2-3 hundred yards out further than our troops had advanced inland.

Only a hundred feet or so from the beach I spotted a small shed with no walls and a thatched palm leaf roof. Machine gun fire came from the shed. I was almost certain that the Jap was manning the m.g. in the shed, but I wasn't positive. I considered there might be some god awful mistake or miscalculation involving our troops instead. However I was 99% sure it was Jap. Cautious, I decided not to fire directly at the spot on the shed's floor where the men and m.g. should be, but instead I elevated the m.g.'s barrel and fired. As I fired I lowered the gun until tracers began to hit the thatched palm roof and set the s.o.b. afire. Done exactly what I wanted to.

Anyhow the m.g. fire from the shed ceased. "Good gunnery," I said to myself. A big beautiful fire was going, no incoming fire from the shed. Gave the nip a hot foot. I knew the fire would get the attention of a BAR man (Browning Automatic Rifleman) and he would take care of the Jap man plenty fine, especially if he ran away from the fire.

There was an incident when we were going out from the beach heading back to the Fuller, *or some other ship to unload the wounded. As we barely left the beach, about 30 feet out, would you believe it? Those damn Japs had set that confounded m.g. up again and were firing into the water only a few feet behind our stern. Hell, we simply out run the m.g. fire, opened up the throttle wide open. Guess the Japs were trying to get me back for setting his damn house on fire ha ha.*

Backing up a bit. As we were going in, in the 15th wave, a guy, a boat coxswain named Peck was coming out from the beach. He had gone in in the 14th wave and had been on the beach when the big shell had exploded in the troops under the palm trees. Shellfire was murderous. He had the craft wide open. His eyes were as wild as a forest boar hog wild. He was crazy with terror. When he got about 30-40 feet away a shell hit the empty well of his boat, exploded in the water after it went through the deck of the craft. [Higgins boat hulls were made of wood.]

We took lots of the blast and shell fragments in the ramp and bow of our craft. To make things worse, his boat suddenly veered to the starboard and smacked us head on doing lots of damage to our bow. He abandoned his sinking craft, and after I loaded the wounded men at the beach where the Jap m.g. fire was, I had to tie up the sinking boat and salvage his radio. We had explicit instructions to do so because it had top secret equipment in the radio. Shellfire was awful, but I managed to salvage the two 30 cal. m.g.s, too.

I started to set a 5 lb. charge of T.N.T. into the craft, but since shellfire was so bad and it was surely sinking I decided against it. That day netted us a Captain's Commendation [from Captain Nathaniel Moore Pigman, USN] for extraordinary bravery in actions. No decorations would be accepted by us all, we informed the Captain. "All in a day's work," we explained to him. He was impressed, and shook hands with us all. Called us all, "son."

Regardless of how well he remembered this incident, it should be remembered that this was J.P.'s fifth invasion and he was still only seventeen years old. As the ship's account relates, the Japanese were on the run and the U.S. Navy was pushing them back to their home islands:

> Events were moving with great rapidity now, and with great forces at the disposal of the high command, there was no delay in making invasion after invasion.

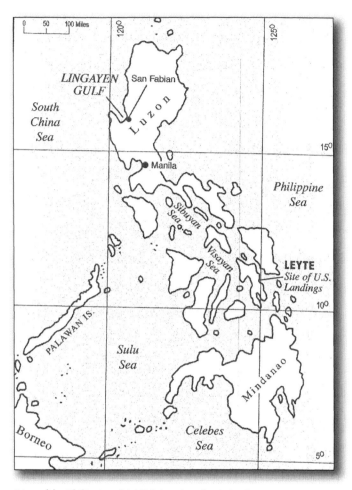

Map of the Philippines highlighting site of U.S. landings at Leyte Gulf.

CHAPTER THIRTEEN

In the Center of the Storm

THE LANDING AT LEYTE GULF PRECIPITATED the largest naval battle in history. J.P. was there and he recounted in detail his part in the operation that saw the effective end of the Japanese fleet:

Harold,

As I promised I will write more about WWII.

After we unloaded our troops on the island of Leyte in the Philippine Islands, it was only a day or two if I remember right 'til the main components of the Japanese battle fleet came in.

I was standing gun watch as a lookout and loader on our starboard 3" gun on the after battery. It was about 1:30 (0130 hours) that things started happening. We and the other ships in our group started moving around. We all got underway and there was a lot of confusion and we almost collided with a couple of ships.

We on the watch knew that something unusual was going on but we had no word from the bridge as to what. *The whole watch was ordered to full alert and we manned our gun and stood a sharp lookout and made ready. After a while all hell broke loose and shells were flying everywhere from warships.* [Note: the largest gun we had at that time was a 3" gun which shot different kinds of shells such as (H.E.) high explosive, amour piercing, (W.P.) white phosphorus, and anti-aircraft.] *The projectiles weighed only 35-40 lbs. and couldn't seriously damage a warship. In a shootout with aircraft we could do pretty well, but in a battle with warships we didn't have the chance of a snowball in hell.*

The Jap battleships had 16" and 18" rifles. Projectiles from these big naval rifles weighed over a ton and maximum range was 25-30 miles. With the puny little 3" guns (four of them) and our anti-aircraft guns we were pretty puny stuff, especially since we had no armor plate for protection.

We and other non-warships had only one chance. That was to slip out of that bottleneck and run for our lives. We did just that. We slipped out while both the warships of the combined Jap and American fleets slugged it out. Sometime later we hugged the shore and sailed south toward Tacloban on the southern tip of Leyte Island. Finally, we reached the comparative safety of the open sea. We spent the next few days sailing around at sea with much of our cargo still in the ship's holds. (We had unloaded our Army and other personnel ashore.)

We escaped the main part of the battle which caused losses aplenty for both sides, much major and minor damage. I don't know how long the battle raged but the Japanese suffered defeat and finally withdrew. Admiral Halsey took off chasing the remainder of the defeated Jap battle fleet. The whole area was left undefended except a few ships such as destroyers, four jeep carriers (i.e. carrier escorts) and some aircraft ashore.

When he chased the Jap fleet north he was about two days away from Leyte when another segment of the Jap battle fleet suddenly appeared back at Leyte Gulf where there was almost no protection. All of Halsey's ships that could have afforded much needed protection for the carrier escorts and DEs (destroyer escorts) and some LSTs (landing ship-tanks). The carriers and shore based planes sprang into action trying to defend the place as much as possible while sending radio messages to Admiral Halsey to return.

All this time we were at sea many miles away from Leyte. We went somewhere and picked up another load of troops, supplies, and equipment for those troops as well as much needed food supplies and ammo for our magazines that fed our AA batteries. For the life of me I can't remember where. It was probably New Guinea or possibly it could have been Espirito Santos in the New Hebrides Islands, a French possession which had many cattle and coconut plantations and which was used as a staging area by Allied forces. Any way we loaded up and sailed back to Leyte.

The ship's account relates that the site was Hollandia, New Guinea, which served as a major re-supply location for ships like the *Fuller*.

J.P. continues:

We arrived very early in the morning just after daybreak. We were at battle stations as we sailed into position to weigh anchor offshore. As we came in we saw several merchant marine ships close to the shore and three Jap planes were making strafing passes at them. I saw no fire from the armed guard's AA guns and most of the convoy except us started firing at the planes. I couldn't understand why we alone were not firing.

I was manning a 30 cal. Machine gun in my boat on the forward deck slightly aft of the forward battery. In a few minutes I noticed one of the planes was hit because it turned away from the merchant ships and sailed into the space between two columns of ships. Flames were streaking along the motor and fuselage. I expected it to explode any minute but it pancaked into the sea and began to break up at the same time it exploded. I could get a good look at it because it was only 100 yards or less away from where I stood.

All of a sudden there appeared an Army P-38 Lockheed Lightning, a two engine twin fuselage fighter which came in forward of the convoy and from the starboard side. It was slightly higher in altitude than the second Jap plane. It dived into a shallow descent firing a burst of 20mm cannon fire, passed over him, and took off after the third Jap plane, who had seen him and turned tail to flee.

For a few seconds I thought he had missed the second Jap plane. Then suddenly, a thin stream of white smoke or steam began to trail out of him. After a few seconds the white smoke turned to black and in a few *more tongues of flame began to lick the fuselage.*

The plane turned at a 90 degree angle and started down the same path as the first plane had gone, in the open space between the columns of ships. He had more altitude and was flying higher than the first. He was probably two or three hundred feet above and he was on fire from stem to stern.

All of a sudden he made another 90 degree turn and started straight for the ship. In fact, straight for where I was. The thought struck me that he was intending to try to ram into us, but he seemed to have too much altitude to be successful at this. Just before he got almost overhead, he exploded into a jillion pieces. I was standing up in my boat in the machine gun turret with only a helmet liner on my head. I had in the excitement, forgot to put on my steel "pot."

All at once a chunk of the wreckage of the plane's explosion zigged by my head, missing only 2 or 3 feet and slammed into the steel deck beside my boat. Boy! I grabbed my steel pot and got my helmet on in a hurry, you bet. I wasn't much scared, just worried that worse to come. ("The little 'rat' kept right on chewing in my guts.")

The third plane had took off running for the island and the P-38 after him. I stood there and watched them until they flew out of sight over the island. A few seconds later I saw an explosion in the air far over the island and I knew the explosion was a plane. I stood there and wondered who got who, the Jap Zero or the P-38.

In a few moments I got my answer. The P-38 Lockheed Lightning came winging back on the same path he had come from and from the looks and action of him he appeared undamaged. Now I knew why we never fired on the first Jap plane in the beginning.

Well, that was that, three Jap planes down in less than ten minutes. There were no more Jap planes and soon we secured from general quarters and began to carry out the ship's work after we ate breakfast, all except those on gun and lookout watches (those men in the engine room and after steering as well as the bridge had watches, too.) The next few days we unloaded troops and their equipment and supplies in the vicinity of Tacloban on the southern tip of the island.

The Jap fleet had been soundly defeated and they had left the area of the Philippines taking their damaged aircraft carriers away and there were no more air raids in the vicinity of Tacloban. There were some airfields on Luzon where the capitol city of Manila was located. The islands of Luzon, Mindanao, and Mindoro had not been taken. There were a number of Jap airfields that sent out observation aircraft and kept briefed on the situation. No Jap war planes interfered with us, however.

From the USS *Fuller's* account:

During our five day run back to Hollandia, the combat ships of the Seventh and Third Fleets intercepted the bulk of the Japanese Navy, and in the now-famous Second Battle of the Philippine Sea, sent their ragged remnants scurrying back to the safety of Japan. The back of Japan's sea power was now broken, and we knew that the worst we now would have to contend with would be her dwindling air force.

With the air above clearing of Japanese planes, J.P.'s youthful nature came forth. Even in war it was hard for him and his pals not to find amusements, and friends. Audrey's comment that "Everyone loved J.P." comes to mind.

He continues:

While unloading equipment in landing craft I got acquainted with a young Filipino girl and got her address, which I lost later on and never did get to write her. She was in a fishing boat with a couple of boys or men which I think were her family.

One of the Army troops aboard ship had a pet monkey who made friends with us, the crew of the ship. He would hop up on everyone's shoulder and when he could get his hands into shirt pockets he would steal your cigarettes, pocket comb, and anything else he could get his hands on and run away. We got to where we couldn't keep anything with him around. They sent a fellow ashore with him and released him into the jungle. (Good riddance.) We never saw him again.

Someone brought a fighting gamecock back to the ship and he ran around on the forward deck for a day or two. One morning he eyeballed Tacloban about a quarter of a mile away and flew off the ship, flew as long as he could, lit in the sea, and swam ashore. I sat and watched him until he hit land. That was the last time we ever saw him.

We stayed around Leyte for a while reinforcing the place, hauling stuff here and there, and finally one fine day we got orders to go back to Pearl Harbor. Fine! Pearl was a long way from war. We could go on liberty, get some beer and drinks, and have a good time. Everyone was happy.

The *Fuller* account shares that a new threat, suicide planes, appeared to join the ever-present submarines.

We left Ataipe on the 28th (of December), in company with U.S.S. *Blue Ridge*, plus units of Task Force 78.1 and escorts. Our trip north as far as Leyte was quiet. We did not stop there, but turned through the passage between Leyte and Mindanao, and entered the Sulu Sea. From this point onward, our force, and the one astern of us were beset by Jap aircraft, which by now had gotten into the habit of making suicide attacks. Japanese submarines were quite active, for in the narrow passages between the islands of the Philippines group, there is marvelous hunting for a well-manned submarine.

Years later, the elderly J.P. recounted what activities meant the most to a still teenaged sailor away from home—a swim, a beer, and a ball game. He continues:

Soon we left Leyte and started back to Pearl Harbor. We stopped at either Kwajalein or Eniwetok in the Marshall atolls and stayed a day or two. Everything was peaceful. The war and the Japs were far away and we had recreation parties ashore. We drank beer, played ball, and went swimming. Me and a fellow crewman swam a mile out to the sea plane anchorage, rested on a raft for about a half hour and swam the mile back. We swam two miles that day in all. We saw several sharks, they were curious but none of them came very close to us. We had a good time drinking beer and swimming that day. I was feeling better and more happy every day I was away from the war. The whole crew was, too.

After a short time in the Marshalls we sailed to Pearl. It took about three days to get there. I thought that if I had time I would visit John Rodgers Airport where I worked in the 10th Naval Transport Squadron, almost 20 miles from Honolulu. I was striker for an aviation machinist, repairing PB2Y bombers which were converted to transport duty, carrying mail and personnel including some VIPs to all points in the south and central [Pacific.] I never got down there. I was too busy visiting bars and seeing the sights in Honolulu.

The day finally came when I could go on liberty. With a nice clean uniform of hand washed to perfection whites I entered a boat to go ashore. I headed to the nearest bar where there was a long line of sailors waiting to go in and have a few beers or mixed drinks or even straight whiskey or gin. I needed a drink bad.

Those Honolulu taxi drivers were a wild bunch. They drive at breakneck speed weaving in and out of traffic, driving all over the road and scaring hell out of their fares. I doubt if there isn't a man who ever rode with a crazy Honolulu taxi driver that didn't do a little praying for his sweet rusty butt.

At this point it is appropriate to ask: Is this a literary diversion by a man still unwilling to address the depth of his alcohol problem? For J.P. the pursuit of alcohol trumped his desire to see old pals where he served prior to assignment on the *Fuller* and, many years later he spins into the mention of the taxi drivers as the reason for his drinking bout.

J.P.'s account continues to describe his use of alcohol as a self-prescribed numbing agent. After all the years he recalls that bottled alcohol was hard to obtain and therefore impossible to smuggle aboard ship:

Well, finally me and a couple of buddies got into the bar. It was nice, clean, and very large for a bar. We all ordered Tom Collins—made with only a little sugar, lime, and gin, plus soda water. They were delicious. We drank at least 4 each before we left, so that some more sailors could get in.

Boy! Was I full of booze, feeling good, back where a torpedo couldn't burst through the side of the ship any minute of the day or night, with my shipmates. I was in Hog Heaven.

This was the life. What luxury. We went on getting a beer or a Tom Collins now and then visiting stores, buying some few things, including picture postcards, getting our pictures taken, even mailing letters that weren't censored. We all had a good time. Late that evening we found a store that had closed and a sailor was locked inside by mistake. We looked for a cop to try to get him out. We never found one. A crowd of people had stopped and we left (shoved off.)

All in all, we had a good time before we went back to the boat landing to catch a LCVP to go back aboard our ship, carrying our smiles and our souvenirs. We were a happy crew. A little booze was

J.P. on liberty with a friend in 1943.

smuggled aboard ship, but I never ever saw a package store where a sailor could buy booze in a bottle.

I got liberty a couple of times and on one occasion I found myself in line for something. I didn't know what. I thought at first it was a movie theater, but as time went on I listened to talk and found out I was in a long line of servicemen to a whorehouse. I thought I would stay in line until a negro fell in line behind me and I said to hell with it. I dropped out of the line and went to another line to a bar, finally got in and got me an icy cold Tom Collins, drank a few, got about half-drunk and decided to find some amusement elsewhere. Went back aboard ship late that night feeling very good.

All of us knew the day would finally come when we would all be aboard ship, underway to go back down south, probably back to the Philippines where the war was still raging.

CHAPTER FOURTEEN

Back in the Fray

NOT YET EIGHTEEN AND GOING BACK FOR YET another invasion, which will earn him a sixth battle star, J.P. has become a well-seasoned veteran with a very real need for alcohol.

Harold,

Will write you a little more about the war.

Well, we enjoyed our stay at Pearl. It was pure luxury to go to sleep at night without worrying that a torpedo might come bursting through the side of the ship and no air raids at anytime.

I developed a taste for Tom Collins mixed drinks and I still love them today. That's drinking lime and gin in style. We all thought we were in hog's heaven when we went to Pearl Harbor. There's not much you can spend money on at sea, except to gamble, and we all could draw several month's pay to blow on anything we chose at Pearl. Besides, being in port for 2-3 weeks is O.K., but after a while a true sailor wants to be back at sea. That's where he is happiest at.

So we stored food, equipment, and troops embarked and we slowly made ready to sail any day. Finally the day came when we were ready and we slipped out of the harbor and soon we were at sea under sealed orders. No one knew where we were going— back to the Philippines and trouble. About three days later we were in the Marshall Islands. We stopped around there at Eniwetok for a day or two and sailed southeast again.

Pretty soon we began to have lectures, and top secret plans for another invasion were unfolded. This time it was the island of Luzon, largest in the Philippines, where the capitol city of Manila was located. There were, if I remember right, about 28,000 Japanese troops on that island, all battle hardened and tough, dangerous as hell.

We went around to a few other places practicing and planning the amphibious landings, studying the top secret plans, learning how to locate the various beaches, for example White Beach 2, Red Beach 3, Black Beach, Blue Beach 1, Gray Beach, Green Beach 2 and so on, landmarks, underwater obstacles, beach defense, mine fields, artillery emplacements, airfields, and everything else that would help, such as barracks placement, general topography of the place and reefs that might pose problems. Navigation at night and so forth. These invasion plans were a complete time table of the push. For example, it might call for an airfield to be constructed on the 4th day after tanks and troops went ashore.

Well, we went around to several places such as Espiritu Santo in the New Hebrides, had a few beers ashore, took combat troops for rest and recreation (R and R), picked up fresh troops and so forth.

We shuttled around all the time. I can't remember just where and when because half the time I forgot what month it was, much less the date. Finally, we were loaded with troops and equipment to make the push with.

As the convoy proceeded we were under constant observation by Jap observation planes. Also, we were under attack several times by Jap torpedo planes and fighter bombers. They did not have enough planes to do a whole lot of damage.

One evening a Jap torpedo plane appeared in the convoy down low about 20-25 feet high aiming for an LSD (landing ship dock) which looked like a war ship with a 5″ gun turret forward. The plane dropped the torpedo and it slewed around, run wild, and missed. Lieutenant Shott pulled out his .45 pistol and shot at the pilot and missed. We laughed about that for days. The torpedo plane stayed down low and got away.

Finally, on our route to Lingayen Gulf on Luzon, we had to go through the strait between Bataan and Corregidor. It was narrow in that strait. Close to shore everywhere. I held my breath because I reasoned that the Japs had shore batteries there, but for one reason or another they never fired on us. They did, however, try to run us aground by broadcasting a radio signal using our code, Del Rio-7, to try to run us and other ships aground. It failed, but the crystal frequency was good. How they managed this I don't know. They were full of tricks as usual. Not only that, Japs were often desperate or suicidal, as we found out on a number of occasions. Also at all times very dangerous.

All the time we were stealing chow and cooking it on hot plates. We stole and ate day and night. Sometimes the cooks gave us stuff to eat and canned shrimp for bait.

Anyhow, to get back on track of the subject at hand, we and the convoy arrived with only one submarine scare. The DEs, DDs, PCs and SCs depth charged the hell out of the place. I don't think they hit anything, but they scared hell out of the Army troops on the ships. They came boiling out of the ships' holds ready to run with nowhere to run to. In a way it was amusing since there wasn't much danger with the escort ships hunting the sub, or subs.

We went to general quarters day and night quite a few times, but like usual most of the time nothing showed up two times out of three. Finally, we entered Lingayen Gulf and anchored off shore. I think the next day was D-day, time to go ashore.

Well, on D-day, early in the morning, we loaded the LCVPs with troops and went into shore where the landing beaches were. We didn't run into much artillery fire. I think we caught the Japs by surprise before they could move a lot of field guns into position.

CHAPTER FIFTEEN

Going Ashore with High Explosives

B ETWEEN HIS PARTICIPATION IN THE TWO INVASIONS of the Philippines J.P. neglects to mention his birthday. Now eighteen years old, he leads a three-man crew on a special mission ferrying high explosives to the beach in the dark. By any standard it is an extremely stressful and very dangerous endeavor for a lad who should be in high school.

He wrote to his son:

Harold,

The last time I wrote about the war we had just made an amphibious landing at Lingayen Gulf on Luzon Island in the Philippines.

Well, after the initial landings we got started hauling more troops and supplies and equipment ashore, both 105mm and 155 mm howitzers plus trucks, jeeps, ammo, water, rations, gasoline, and crates of Bangalore torpedoes. (A piece of brittle hardened pipe about 8 feet long, filled with pentalite, (pentaerythritol tetranitrate) a very high powered high explosive, which could cut down barb wire or concertina wire surrounding bunkers, pill boxes, and other military installations. The pipe put out tiny pieces of shrapnel so intense that it cut through barb wire like a hot knife through butter.

Well, we worked day and night with very little sleep or rest, hauling stuff into the beach. Air raids were common occurrences although the Japs threw most of their air power at the battle fleet units and left us in a relative position of some safety free to carry out our operations. Small boats like landing craft were seldom bothered with air attacks upon them.

After a while the Japs brought up artillery and it got dangerous to haul stuff ashore. I stole a half case of hand grenades so we could have more protection against suicidal Jap swimmers. I also built a little diesel oil stove out of odds and ends to make hot chocolate and coffee. This kept our rations warm, although we could heat rations cans on the boat engine's manifold.

One night the boat officer came up and wanted a crew to deliver a load of Bangalore torpedoes ashore. He explained that the shell fire was intense ashore and that he wouldn't order any one to go, only volunteers. I called up my engineer and bow hook and explained the situation to them, telling them I was willing to volunteer if they were. Although the shell fire was so intense that we might all be signing our death warrants by going.

They volunteered to go.

I told the Officer of the Deck, whom I called Long John when we were out of earshot of everyone else. I shook hands with him because we both knew this might be the last time we saw one another on this earth. Soon we were loaded and the bow hook shoved off the LCVP and we were underway with the Bangalores going to shore.

On the way we had a couple of scares. Our star shells, which the destroyers shot up to illuminate the battle grounds, some of these were duds and fell short close to us. It's a scary thing seeing a big ball of fire coming straight at you. They all fell short of us, maybe a hundred yards or more away.

Scary as hell.

After a while we began to come into shell fire. The closer to shore we went, the more intense was the artillery barrage. Shells were exploding all around us and I was afraid we would go up if one exploded on top of us. It wasn't the shell fire that bothered us as much as it was the tons of sensitive high explosives we had on board.

Finally, I called a halt and told the engineer and bow hook to gather around and consult. There wasn't a glimmer of light ashore. That meant that even if by some miracle we got ashore with the load intact, we couldn't get unloaded. Also, closer to the shore we could see the shells were coming in so hot and heavy, so much that it seemed the whole ocean was exploding. Hundreds of shells a minute were slamming in.

I said we could take a vote on it, but I thought it would be sheer suicide to attempt a landing and even by some miracle we made it in, we could not get unloaded, and not a light anywhere.

Well, they voted to back off and wait 'til morning to

try to go in. After we got back out of the shell fire, anchored, and worked out a schedule of posting watch, I loaded the port machine gun (30 cal.) because the night before a boat had drifted close to an enemy held beach and got themselves in a fire fight with Jap troops ashore. After that we kept one man on watch, rotated every two hours while the rest slept. So passed the night.

The next morning I was on watch. Just before daybreak at our stern a string of tracers, a twin pair of them, started slamming into the water. As I watched them getting closer and closer, I first thought a boat was firing on the horizon and they were lobbing over to us.

I hit the deck. I realized by this time that it was a plane, although I could not see him or hear him. The tracers were coming from the sky. Something in me said, "Damn your soul, Nunnally, get off your damn belly and fight like a man!"

So I grabbed the 30 m.g. that I had loaded the night before, cocked it and pulled the trigger—nothing! I cocked it again, all the time screaming for my crew to wake up. Tracers hit in the water only inches from the boat, making a sizzling sound like pouring water on a red hot stove. My heart was in my mouth. I knew that if one of those tracers hit in several tons of high explosives we were carrying we would all be nothing but a bloody mist in less than a second. As the tracers slammed into the water I thought, "Pretty little devils, but deadly."

The strings of tracers passed us and hit one or two LSTs close to shore, and started a few small fires. I was pretty shook up, not from the m.g. attack, but of the fact that we were carrying several tons of Bangalore torpedoes.

Eventually it got light enough so we could see the shore. The shelling has stopped and people were moving around. We beached the boat and before long we unloaded our cargo, and I breathed a sigh of profound relief. I backed that boat off the beach and we got underway to go back to the ship. We pulled up close to an LCI and when we were about 20 yards away a shell zipped over the LCI and hit about 100 yards in front of it. I snorted in contempt. It was evident the Japs were trying to hit the LCI but missed by a wide margin. The next moment a shell hit square in the forward 40mm AA turret and 2 or 3 sailors jumped over the side with their clothes on fire. I started over to fish them out of the water, but an officer on the LCI waved us off. He was already slowing down to pick them up. Chalk up one for the Japs.

We went back to the ship unharmed thanks to the Good Lord or the gods of war, whichever. Well as it turned out, the reason I never got a shot off at the Jap plane is that I had not loaded the 30 cal. m.g. properly. And the plane? It had simply cut off its engine and glided in silently, hence no sound. So much for that.

SAILOR MAN

CHAPTER SIXTEEN

Shenanigans on Shore

J.P. RECOUNTED MORE ABOUT HIS LIFE ON BOARD and ashore. Some is informative and some disturbing. All of it points at a case of PTSD being self-treated with alcohol:

Harold, son,

Well in the last letter I wrote you about the Jap aircraft attack on my landing craft. Thinking it over, the Jap pilot may have just been strafing the beach or the two LSTs and maybe I was just in his way. He may not have even seen me.

Scary anyhow. Boy! Just one of those tracer slugs hitting several tons of high explosive Bangalore torpedoes might have set off an explosion of such magnitude that probably not even a hair on my head would have been found. The boat would have been only pieces and splinters. At any rate, neither you nor I would be alive today. Scary as hell.

Anyhow, we settled down to work hauling supplies ashore. We worked day and night. The Japs sent a few aircraft over now and then, but the shelling of the beaches finally petered out. The troops ashore were making pretty good progress at hacking up the Jap army.

A "bit of home" takes place three days after his eighteenth birthday of December 22nd and J.P. explains how drinking money is made available through his ingenuity.

He wrote:

Sometime along about this time it was Christmas Day 1944. We really had a feast, everything, turkey and ham, everything from soup to nuts. I mean nuts. We had 5 gallon cans of mixed nuts, and they were really good. Lord, I never before or since ate such a grand style meal at Xmas.

The Philippines Campaign was going fine. Manila was liberated and we got to go on liberty 2 or 3 times in Manila. I was in the black market business in a small way. I took two cartons of cigarettes ashore to sell. I got enough out of them to have a good time that evening. I went to a popular bar called the Piggly Wiggly and two pretty Filipino girls came to set and drink and dance with us. They were friendly and good company. We enjoyed ourselves immensely, decked out in dress whites we were in the lap of luxury that day. I think maybe the whole island was secured and mopped up of the Japanese, but I am not sure about that. I guess maybe the campaign on Luzon was about over

By this time the monsoon was over, thank the good Lord. We stayed high off Philippine booze and dry, too. Philippine booze was raw stuff, but it was plenty strong.

J.P.'s interests are typical for a young male and at times go beyond alcohol:

We were still hauling some stuff, except in lesser quantities than before. I got liberty several more times and decided to visit a Filipino "cat house." The second one I visited. Me and a young pretty Filipino girl were upstairs on a bamboo floor fooling around when a guy came in with a service .45 auto in his hand. He didn't pay any attention to me and the girl, but was walking around like he expected to find someone up there. Of course the place was empty, except me and the girl and my buddy Savage and his girl. He didn't speak, but walked around staring at the walls and then went back down the stairs without a word spoken.

I have wondered about him since. Was he a cop, or what? Why the .45 auto? He was a Filipino. Maybe he was a member of the Philippine Constabulary. Who knows? Even today I wonder.

By this time J.P.'s behavior on liberty is totally wrapped up in obtaining the numbing effect of alcohol. The negative consequences of his actions are ignored, minimalized, or the source material for humor, which is common in the mind of a PTSD sufferer avoiding the pain of recollection. J.P. continues:

Another liberty party I was on ended with bad results. Me and my buddy Savage got a court martial out of it.

We started out at the Piggly Wiggly Bar, me and Savage got almost drunk. As we walked down the street, it was muddy as all get out from a rain that day, an argument started between me and him. In a minute I smacked him flat on his back in the mud. Reaching under his arms, I stood him back on his feet and knocked him down again. I did this several times, and then a Filipino man grabbed my sleeve and said, "Please don't hit him again!"

I stopped and about this time the Shore Patrol arrived in a jeep, an officer and an enlisted man. They arrested us and loaded us into the jeep and drove us away to the old Filipino prison where they had a S. P. station. On the way Savage got good and mad at me, hit me in the nose and broke it. I bled like a stuck frog.

All along the ride to the S.P. station I was thinking how good it would be to escape. That was all I could think about "escape." We arrived at the S.P. station. It was on the inside of a fence. The S.P.s took us to a small prison where they booked us on a number of charges.

Well, they booked my buddy Savage and left me in the building by myself while they put him in a cell. While I sat there the word "escape" kept popping in my mind. I walked out the door and started running for the fence surrounding the old prison. They seen me running and hollered to S.P.s up the way to head me off.

Soon they caught me and all three proceeded to beat the hell out of me, two holding me while a third whammed me in the gut until he wore himself out.

Then he would take turns holding me while the other two slammed me in the gut. All of the S.P.s done me in proper. My legs felt like strings. I couldn't even walk to the cell. They had to half help me, half carry me. Boy, I had the hell beat out of me proper and good. A beautiful job they done on me. I knew that because at times I had been a Shore Patrolman myself. I had had to arrest drunks occasionally myself. Sometimes I even carried a gun, a .38 Smith & Wesson owl head or a .45 service auto. I had worked for them and done like now, got drunk, got in trouble, and arrested by them.

Well, to make a long story short, they tossed seven of us into a dark cell. Sometime during the night all of us got into a gang fight. Sometime during the night also I found a small trap door in the floor of the cell. Escape was still on my mind. I tried to crawl out the trap door in the floor, which turned out to be the toilet.

The next day I awoke to find shit in my hair, in my eye brows, and mixed with mud and blood, all over my white dress uniform. God what a shitty mess. I smelled like hell, too. God what a wild drunk.

Sometime the next day we got out of jail. We had eaten something and got a cigarette after each meal. That night I had cleaned up, took a bath, eaten, and got a good night's sleep aboard the good ole USS Fuller. *Home sweet home.*

A few days later me and Savage stood on the bridge facing a Deck Court Martial. Our lawyers and the Captain were there. It was a short trial. I got 20 days brig time, 60 days restriction to the ship, $144 fine,

200 hours extra duty, and a threat to send me to Mare Island Naval Penitentiary if I got into any more trouble. End of story.

Nothing can be added to this story. J.P.'s drinking has gotten out of hand. When not involved in activities aimed at relieving stress, he is aboard ship, where he encounters a mixture of boredom, stress and danger.

CHAPTER SEVENTEEN

Lucky Lady

Activities that were "over the line" were not always restricted to the enlisted ranks. J.P. and his pals shared their good fortune with an enterprising young officer who was more than willing to enjoy the spoils of war.

Harold,

More about the episodes that I experienced in WWII.

Well, as I wrote before our work in the Philippines was almost done. One evening I ran into what the most homesick boat coxswains would have considered pure heaven. It was a really big barge pulled up close to shore. I circled around looking it over. Beer in cases was stacked up higher than my head. I found out later that it had about 50,000 cases of beer on it! Enough to fill a large warehouse.

I turned my LCVP over to my engineer and told him to pull alongside the barge and tie up to it. I went up on the deck and walked around the stacks of beer trying to locate the guard who I knew was bound to be around somewhere. I walked around the stern section and peeked around the corner to the starboard side. About halfway down the side I saw him. He was drunk as a loon.

I ducked down and retreated back across the stern section and back about one third of the port section to where my boat was tied up by my engineer and bow hook crewman. "All clear," I said to them and began tossing cases of beer into the boat.

Suddenly, I heard a noise somewhere on the barge. I jumped into the boat with a case of beer in my hands. Dived in would have been a better word. "Let's get the hell out of here," I yelled to my crew, "that S.O.B. has got a loaded M1 rifle!" we took off like a bat out of hell. Our work was about done for the day.

Late that evening all of us in the pool got together and tied up together and dropped our anchors and made preparations to post rotating watches for the night. I counted the beer. We had 13 cases of beer! Some of the other boats had stolen beer, too. Some even more than we. Boy! Talk about having a beer party! We really had a time that night.

The next night, so much beer had been stolen by then the officers decided to have a locker search to see if any of the beer had been brought aboard the ship. They passed the word over the P.A. system for each of the crewmen to open and stand beside his locker for inspection. We had 4 cases of beer in my boat that I knew we had to get out and hide because after the locker inspection there might be boat inspection, too.

I gathered up my crew and we were standing on the after part of the promenade deck discussing ways and means to get the beer aboard and hide it, when a *young Ensign we knew overheard us, and he said, "If you boys got anything you want to keep out of sight bring it down to my cabin. It will be safe there."*

"O.K. and thanks!" we told him. "We will split 50-50 with you."

"Fine," he said.

A few moments later we smuggled the beer aboard and stored it in that young officer's cabin. They never missed our not opening our lockers and standing by them. Probably thought we were either on watch or was off on a boat trip. We had nothing in our lockers anyhow—got off Scott Free. We gave the Ensign two cases and kept two. Everyone was happy.

Meanwhile, our daily routine was almost as safe as peacetime.

The ship's account recounts how the fabled ship and its veteran crew worked at this landing:

Standing into transport area Able off San Fabian, and swung into routine of the "Amphibs." The first wave of troops left the ship at 1056, followed by two waves leaving at one minute intervals and hit the beach without too much opposition, thanks to the accuracy of the bombardment. We remained in Lingayen that night, getting little sleep, due to the almost constant pressure of suicide aircraft over the gulf, and to the fact that we still had some cargo to unload, not having received our unloading orders until late in the evening. We had completed debarkation by daylight, despite the interruptions, and were able, on the tenth, to retire from the area with our group. For the prompt unloading of the ship during difficult conditions, and in such short time, Captain Pigman was awarded a citation from 7th Fleet.

J.P. saw it this way. He continues:

A backward glance at the invasion of Luzon at Lingayen Gulf...our group of APAs and AKAs suffered some damage and loss at the gulf that I forgot to mention, since damage is so commonplace in war, sometimes almost a daily occurrence.

During the last week or so at the gulf, Jap torpedo boats had been coming out of a river on Luzon out in the gulf harassing ships at night. It got where it was somewhat dangerous for small boats such as LCMs and LCVPs to work at night. Several were fired upon by ships in the gulf including a couple of boat coxswain friends of mine. Although we gave recognition signals with battle lanterns and flashlights with colored paper under the lens, it didn't always work.

Sometimes we had air raids at night also. Sometimes I fired the .30 cal. m.g. up in the air where the tracers from the ships and boats around me were going, a waste of good ammunition. The gun was too small to be very effective against a Jap warplane, about the same as a slingshot.

The USS *War Hawk* was an AP transport (#168) of the La Salle class, with only eight Higgins boats. The USS *DuPage* was a Bayfield class APA (#41). It lost thirty-five men in the attack, with an additional 136 men being wounded.

An account follows of what happened to the *War Hawk*:

On the morning of 10 January 1945, *War Hawk* was anchored in Lingayen Gulf where she was attacked in the dark by a "Shinyo" suicide boat. These boats were small motorboats laden with up to two tons of explosives in the bow. Lookouts reported hearing an approaching boat when the Shinyo rammed the port side of the ship. The explosion blew a 25 foot hole in hold number three killing 61 men. (Commander Thompson's official Action Report filed on 18 January 1945 states that 23 people were missing and unaccounted for 20 minutes after the explosion. He does not give details on the wounded.) The damage to the ship was extensive including flooding in the engine room which knocked out power. With the ship dead in the water, the crew struggled to keep her afloat, restore power and fight off continuing Japanese air attacks throughout the day.

J.P. describes the action:

Anyhow, the gulf, like Leyte was a bottleneck. The night before we left, the USS DuPage *and the USS* War Hawk *a couple of APAs in our group had attempted to slip undetected. They failed. Jap torpedo boats had engaged them further up the gulf, torpedoed the USS* War Hawk *which the Captain ran aground to keep the ship from sinking.*

The DuPage *was run back to the main body where we were. Fire and explosions on the stern of the War Hawk chased part of the crew forward. They had built a wooden catwalk over the hatch of an open hold and the explosion had wrecked it. In the dark men fell all the way down the dark hold. Many of them died in the fall and I guess many were seriously injured. The total casualty count on the* War Hawk *was said to be 65 men dead and injured. We all felt sad for them.*

The next evening about dusky dark the main convoy attempted to leave. [Also it was three days later that the *War Hawk* downed a suicide plane.] *The USS* DuPage *was column leader, running 500 feet ahead of us. We were at battle stations because we were in the midst of an air raid when suddenly the tracers from our forward battery anti-aircraft guns began to criss-cross in the air. I knew then that a Jap plane was almost on top of us.*

The *DuPage* was not lucky in taking a suicide plane's hit. The ship's account tells how J.P. and the *Fuller* luckily escaped being the target:

Due to a last minute change in plan, we were relieved as column leader by the DuPage. At 1917 one enemy aircraft was sighted dead ahead coming in low and at 1918 this plane was seen to crash into the DuPage. The DuPage was lit up momentarily by a tremendous explosion. There were many casualties. Survivors were sighted in the water, and we, as well as the ships following us, maneuvered to avoid these, meanwhile dropping life jackets and rings to those in the water.

J.P. explains:

I wasn't on a gun at general quarters. I was standing on the after quarterdeck starboard side with a bucket of sand to put out any fuel oil fires that might crop up. I was talking to Chief Petty Officer Nittaraur, our division petty officer.

All at once Nittaraur started to run. I hit the deck immediately, then the sky lit up in a pink light, then I heard the sound of an explosion. I said to myself, My God, we have been hit up forward!" As it turned out, the USS DuPage, 500 feet ahead of us, had took a Jap twin engine suicide bomber with a full bomb load.

Men in the water started coming by on the port side of the ship. The water was full of them hollering for help. We threw a bunch of life rafts with water and food attached to them overboard for them to float on. It is my belief that some of the men simply saw the plane coming, couldn't get out of the way, and jumped over the side to escape injury. I suppose destroyers and patrol craft picked them up later.

The next day we took medicine and medical personnel over to the USS DuPage while at sea. She had dropped out of position as column leader and she was now in place on our port beam, a position reserved for the USS Monrovia an APA [#31] which was now column leader ahead of us.

There were many sailors badly burned in that attack. A chief petty officer on the DuPage said all the bombs had exploded on the Jap plane except two, and they had rolled those over the side. I never did find out how many dead were on the DuPage. We all felt very sorry for the men on the other ships which in a sense we considered them almost as our own shipmates. So there it is. One ship of our group lost and one badly damaged at Lingayen Gulf.

Again, in his matter-of-fact style, J.P. downplays the danger of duty aboard an attack transport. Since the first Allied invasion in the South Pacific at Guadalcanal in 1942, where APAs were the target of the initial Japanese counter-attack, APAs were in constant danger. The result was that J.P. spent months, if not years, at the cutting edge of battle and was therefore susceptible to the causes PTSD.

CHAPTER EIGHTEEN

Greenhorns with Guns

T HE POSSIBILITY OF GETTING HIT BY FRIENDLY FIRE is a reality in combat. The following observation from an old "seasoned salt" is interesting and illuminating, as it comes from eighteen-year-old J.P.

Harold,

In the latter part of the war we got a lot of green, trigger-happy scared men. They were dangerous to everybody. They would shoot at everything that moved at night. We had to haul troops and supplies all night long. Me, and about all the other Boat Coxswains I knew, had been shot at one or more times, sometimes with anti-aircraft 20mm cannon. Shell splinters from exploding 20mm isn't any fun to deal with.

We had recognition signals with flash lights with colored tissue paper under the lenses and a sequence of dots and dashes. We always too had pass words and phrases, but nothing made any difference to the green scared trigger happy bastards, they fired away.

The decks of all the ships had riflemen standing guard on the deck during invasions. Some were armed with submachine guns, others with '03 rifles, also pistols (45 auto) and .38 revolvers, M77 "grease guns," and carbines. It was dangerous to approach any ship without recognition signals, but those green horns would sometimes fire on you no matter how much you signaled. We got to where we fired back at the scared bastards. If you fired back on them those cowards quit firing every time.

Well, back to the vicinity of Manila on Luzon. I was still in the black market business in a small way—cigarettes, shoes, and mattress covers were the preferred items. I think they ripped mattresses apart and used the cloth to make other things like shirts and blouses out of the cloth. Size 7 shoes were in high demand. The Filipinos must have had small feet. You could sell a few size 8s, but not many. The local Filipino liquor was still $2.00 per fifth. We drank a lot of it.

About this time they came out with our Amphibious Forces shoulder patch. It was on a blue and red background with crossed submachine guns on a navy anchor. It was beautiful. By this time I had served in the 3rd, 5th, and 7th Amphibious Forces and I wore it with pride, but only on blue dress uniform. Down in the Pacific we only wore dress whites.

Well, demand for our work fell off. Mindanao and Mindoro had been secured by U.S. forces by this time and the Jap air base had been closed down. No more worry about Jap air raids. Then too, the Jap fleet, the remainder of it, had long left to get repairs at home bases on the Japanese mainland and other far off places. It began to be peacetime in Manila.

I still frequented the Piggly Wiggly Bar in Manila, dancing with and talking with the girls who worked there, having a very good time. One fine day the atmosphere aboard ship was electrified. We had just received word that we had just been ordered back to the states. Boy! We were one crew of happy sailors.

In a day or two we cleared the harbor at Manila underway for first the Marshalls and then Pearl Harbor and eventually the good ole U.S. of A. We had a happy voyage every foot of the way. We drank what hooch we had stored, stole everything that wasn't nailed down, gambled, listened to the juke box in the mess hall and had a hell of a good time.

Back at Pearl Harbor, and also on the way home, young J.P. parties to numb his mind and memory of combat:

We were all in high spirits eagerly awaiting liberty ashore, and soon after we dropped anchor and a group of us went ashore. I headed for an old familiar bar and downed about five Tom Collins drinks in a row. God! What luxury. No work to do, no fear of enemy aircraft, no chance of being torpedoed, no chance of running into an enemy battle fleet.

Half-drunk with money in my pocket, beautiful women working in barbershops and stores. What a glorious life! What luxury.

I walked and staggered to another bar and tanked up again. I wanted to make a bet with someone that

I could drink all the booze in Honolulu. Nobody would bet with me. Hell, they thought if anybody could do it, I could. When I, by some miracle, got back to the ship nothing worked about me except my mouth, and it didn't work good. It only croaked when I would try to talk. Next day, I had a beautiful hangover and was thoroughly ashamed of myself for getting so blasted into space.

After several days of boozing, working, and what not, we weighed anchor and sailed toward the States. It was a joyous voyage. Everyone was in high spirits, even the officers lightened up on us, giving us friendly glances, striking up conversations with us, and so on. After about six days at sea we entered the bay at San Francisco and sailed under the Golden Gate Bridge. I wouldn't have trade places with anyone on earth.

In San Francisco, J.P.'s abuse of alcohol continues. He writes:

We had a ship's dance. The ship's welfare fund paid $20,000 for two of them at The Club Lido on 915 Columbus Avenue in downtown San Francisco. Everyone had a good time. Only time in my life that I ate squab (pigeon). A fine meal that cost twenty bucks a plate. (In those days about a hundred dollars equivalent today.)

This next passage says a lot about the work ethic of the men from this era—they are home from combat and picking up extra jobs.

We went into Moore's dry dock for overhauling. We could soon go on liberty every night while the first half of the crew went home on leave. Some of the other guys had nothing to do aboard ship and they got jobs ashore to make some extra money. Some of them worked tending bars, others worked in the shipyards and stores. At that time I worked in the mess hall and I could only work at night ashore. Instead, I went on liberty every night instead of working.

Finally, I was to go home. My leave papers were issued to me and having spent so much money on liberty at night in Frisco, I had to borrow 70 bucks for train fare.

J.P. wanted to go home, but he also wanted to drink and had spent his liberty time drinking away his pay.

Soon I was off, entrained via the overland route through the central longitudinal expanse of the U.S. We passed through Nevada, Colorado, Flag Staff Arizona, Nebraska, Kansas, Missouri, and finally into Memphis, Tennessee. I bought some booze in Memphis, left there late at night and arrived in Birmingham early in the morning.

Before I opened my eyes I knew I was in Alabama from the smell of the air. The air smells different in Alabama than anywhere else. Good ole home sweet home! Soon I was on the bus for home. I had acquired a Jap rifle, which I sling over my shoulder in the manner of an infantryman and headed for the

Purefoy Hotel when I arrived in Talladega. My brother, L.J., worked there.

Soon I was shaking hands and patting on the shoulder of my brother whom I had not seen in approximately two years. It was certainly good to see the old boy again. Later that evening, we caught a bus and headed for Ledbetter Crossing.

Finally we arrived at home for a joyous reunion with mother, my sister Audrey, and my other brothers, William, Clyde, and Marvin. It was a joyous time, eating home cooked meals that my mother prepared. Everyone was happy. The whole family was together again.

Mother and Daddy had killed a hog and had a large ham in the kitchen. For some reason my Daddy never smoked hams, only curing them in salt or Morton's sugar cure. It was very good anyhow. Daddy and the boys had robbed several wild bee trees and plenty of honey was around the place. Later, after I got out of the service, all of us robbed about thirty-one wild bee trees one year and hived three swarms in wooden hives that we built. We kept them and robbed them around June 10th each year and had honey the year around. We still robbed wild bees, too.

Well, time went fast and soon I was in route back to Frisco and the ship and crew that I had learned to love almost as much as home.

I arrived back at Frisco and resumed duties aboard ship. A lot of work had been done. We now had four twin 20mm anti-aircraft guns, instead of single 20s. We still had some single AA guns left on the boat deck, 20mms that is. Lots of improvement in gunnery, and other parts of the ship had benefited. All of the old paint had been sand blasted off the hull and repainted. It was said that the total bill by Moore's exceeded $1,000,000.

Soon we must sail for God knows where in the Pacific. Final preparations were being made to sail, all the crew was back aboard the ship. Finally, the day came, the P.A. system squawked, "Now hear this! All hands make preparation to get underway. Engine room, light boilers #2 and #4."

Slowly, we sailed out of Frisco bay into the open Pacific. Soon we were past all the mooring buoys and at sea.

This is all for now, Harold.

Next Okinawa.

SAILOR MAN

CHAPTER NINETEEN

Headed to a
Giant Ruckus

A FTER A COMPLETE OVERHAUL THE USS *FULLER* returned to participate in the largest invasion of the Pacific war. At eighteen J.P. earns his seventh battle star.

Harold,

Will write a little more about WWII.

Leaving the USA behind, we sailed to Pearl Harbor. The trip was uneventful, the green troops we were transporting all got seasick and they were laying around on the forward deck sick as all get out. The first division seamen turned fire hoses on them and washed them as well as the deck down with water. They had vomited all over themselves and the deck, too. Seasickness is about the most sick a man can get and not be in danger of his life. I got broke in on my first voyage in calm water and didn't suffer too much.

A number of crap games were going on, but I had to stay out of them because I had spent all the money I drew out of my pay at Frisco. We ate good because we had fresh milk, eggs, and produce we picked up in the states. Meat too, good and fresh stuff. A few days later we arrived at Honolulu, Pearl Harbor.

We got liberty a few times dressed in whites, a very neat and pretty summer dress uniform. I rambled around the city quite a lot. Got a haircut by a woman barber and drank a good many Tom Collins at 40 cents per drink.

I had a lot of mixed feelings. The war was going good for us, but, my God, it might last another couple of years. The Japanese were cleared out of the Philippines by then, but there were places like Formosa (Taiwan) and large parts of China, all of French Indochina, Korea, Manchuria besides the home islands like Honshu, Hokkaido, Kyushu, and the rest, where the jap was entrenched and tough as they came. Also, they were on Okinawa, only 300 miles from the Jap homeland island of Honshu.

We left Pearl and headed back to the Philippine Islands via Eniwetok in the Marshall atolls. We stopped at Eniwetok for a while, then we set sail for Manila. We were in the convoy with numerous other ships of all kinds and descriptions, plus our escort vessels such as SCs, PCs, and destroyers (DDs.)

When we arrived at Manila, Top Secret War dept. documents were out and we began to study them along with the boat officer, whose name I forget. I think there were about 28,000 Jap troops on the island. What worried us most was that it was within easy aircraft range from the home islands. We went over the map of the island studying the topography, the reefs and rivers, planned landing sites and things like mine fields and underwater obstacles and such things as artillery emplacements, barracks, the towns and villages. In short the whole Enchilada.

We practiced with machine guns at floating targets 1,000 yards away. Try hitting one of these at 1,000 yards in a rocking boat, ha. No chance. We practiced fake runs on friendly beaches and practiced stripping down a .30 cal. m.g. I managed to strip down a .30 cal. and put it back together, ready to fire, in 22 minutes, a good run, in a short time.

Well, we talked, discussed, and planned and practiced some more, 'til finally we felt we were ready for Freddy. Full speed ahead!

We got liberty a few times in Manila and on the first trip I headed back to the ole Piggly Wiggly Bar and Grill in hopes of seeing an on old friend, a girl who worked there. I got to see her, she was dancing with some sailor. She was glad to see me , but I was so blind drunk that she didn't want to dance with me. Besides, she was playing hostess for another sailor. I had a drink and left for elsewhere. I felt like dunking my head in a bucket of cold water until I sobered up.

Well, we and other amphibious ships shuttled around from place to place in the Philippines gathering up combat troops and equipment for the trip to Okinawa. We ended up with part of the 15th Marine Air Wing, which, along with the help of Navy CBs (construction battalions) were supposed to get an air strip into operational condition on the 4th day after D-day. They did exactly that, I learned later.

Pretty soon all the ships headed to Okinawa put to sea. God! What an Armada. More ships in that convoy than I could imagine even existed. Warships, carriers, battleships, cruisers, destroyers, and dozens of other types of ships, including APAs, PAs, AKAs, minesweepers, LSTs, and LCIs. God! What a convoy to throw against the Jap Empire including its suicide pilots and kamikaze aircraft. Somebody was going to have a heyday. As it turned out it was a giant ruckus costing the navy about 30 ships and a loss of life for some 4,000 navy men, as well as about 8,000 marines and army troops.

My main worry was that Ole J.P. Skinny Ass Nunnally, weighing a puny 173 lbs., was heading straight to hell right smack in the middle of it all. I spent lots of time wishing I was far away. It seemed to me like I was overdue for a piece of hot shell fragment with my number on it. I had watched too many good men buried by dumping them over the side of the ship I was on weighted down with sand in a canvas bag. I had took too many chances and I had too many thousands of pieces of shell fragments screaming around me. I was going to get it but good.

I began to set around deck late at night when I was not on watch. Most of my thoughts were about getting hit, or even death. I wondered about heaven and hell, and finally decided I didn't know a damn thing about religion and I doubted if anyone else knew either. Besides, I wasn't sure if I even believed in religion or heaven or hell, and about the best a drunk whore hopper like me could expect was a bunk in that ship which sailed that great and glorious slime pit in the sky.

Finally I quit thinking about stuff like that, deciding if I get it. That's too damn bad. Besides, I was a military man and it's all in the game and a day's work for anyone in the U.S. Militia.

Just to be on the safe side, I drew out $300 back pay and mailed it to my mother. She could well use it with the other money I had sent her along for a couple of years past.

We had a long sail to Okinawa, plenty of hard work keeping the ship shipshape and everything squared away and too a lot of time spent on watches. I was port wing lookout then working on the port wing of the bridge, equipped with binoculars and a set of battle phones. I was sort of an assistant to the quartermaster and the Officer of the Deck. I relayed all the messages coming out of the bridge over phone to all gun batteries, all lookout watches on the flying bridge and the fore and aft crow's nest, and called for changes of speed to the engine room.

In short, I was in phone contact with all the points of the ship and relayed all outgoing messages to different points as directed by the Officer of the Deck (acting Captain of the ship) and relayed all incoming messages from gun batteries, engine room, after steering etc. back to the Officer of the Deck.

Sometimes I stayed mighty busy handling all these outgoing and incoming messages. I stared out at the sea through the glasses one day and spotted a strange looking vessel a long way distant, almost on the horizon. I called the O.D.'s attention to it. In a few minutes an aircraft carrier in the middle of the convoy put up planes which attacked the strange vessel, which put up anti-aircraft fire to the diving planes, who were strafing it and dropping bombs trying to hit it.

I don't know whether they sank it or not, nor did I ever find out if my alert to it caused the signalmen to signal the aircraft carrier before they proceeded to put up aircraft to attack it. Quien Sabe? (Who Knows).

We were under constant observation by Japanese aircraft. We shot down numerous Jap observation planes. The convoy did, not us, the "Fuller." We never got a chance to shoot. The Jap planes were more interested in the warships than troop transports like us.

One day a very strange thing happened. A heavy cruiser, the USS Indianapolis pulled alongside of us and we started taking powder charges and 8" shells aboard. We, the crew, gave each other looks as the cruiser continued to unload ammunition intended for her own 8 inch gun batteries. After she unloaded many shells and powder charges she left the convoy and headed back the way we came from, to God knows where. This was a most puzzling situation and it wasn't until long after the war was over that I found out the answer to that puzzle.

The USS Indianapolis was called back to the states to pick up the first atom bomb parts and transport them to Tinian Island for the B-29 bombers located there to drop them on the city of Hiroshima in Japan. What a puzzle. We never saw the cruiser again. She was sunk by a Jap submarine a few days before the war ended in the Philippines, that is the Philippine Islands.

There is another interesting link between the *Fuller* and the *Indianapolis*. Commodore Theiss, the ship's well known first captain, served on the court martial of Captain Charles B. McVay III, who was convicted of failing to zig zag the course of his ship. That action may not have contributed to the torpedoing of the *Indianapolis*, yet McVay was held accountable anyway. The guilty verdict may have been in reaction to the fact that the death of 583 crewmembers during and following the attack, primarily to sharks, was the greatest single loss of life in the history of the U.S. Navy.

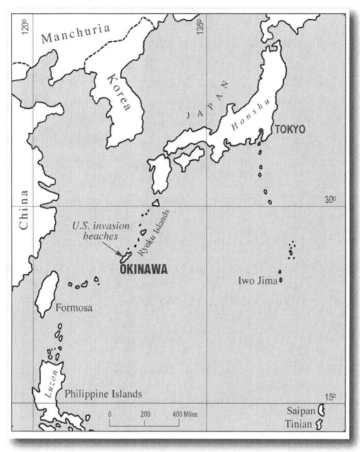

Map showing position of the island of Okinawa in relation to Japan.

CHAPTER TWENTY

Terror on Okinawa

F OLLOWING CONCENTRATED SUICIDE ATTACKS FROM the air Okinawa proved to be a drawn out bloody battle that provided the U.S. a terrifying example of what an invasion of the Japanese home islands would be like.

Harold,

Finally came the day we came in sight of Okinawa. Cruisers, destroyers, and battleships were cruising up and down the coast softening up Jap defenses. Flights of Navy Corsair and Hell Cat fighter bombers were headed inland in search of targets. There was lots of activity. Radio traffic, both American and Japanese picked up to a fever pitch and even a fool could have told plenty was going on and more to follow. Our job as usual was to repel Japanese aircraft, load out boats with troops, supplies, and equipment and send them ashore as safely as we could, and of course, avoiding the artillery shelling which was sure to follow. We hoped it would be light.

D-day finally came early one morning sometime in August. I watched assault troops (Marine Corps) climbing down into boats from debarking cargo nets draped over the sides of ships. The whole damned procedure seemed unreal to me, like it was some movie instead of real life.

We loaded our troops and headed ashore. I was not coxswain this time. My friend Abernathy was. I was to take charge of the boat later to relieve him. For once I did not have Merriata in the craft with me as engineer. He was on a tank lighter, and LCM and was late instrumental in shooting down a Jap war plane with a .50 Cal machine gun. He done a fine job at it.

As we were about half way to shore, two or three artillery shells exploded as they hit the water. It suddenly occurred to me, I didn't have my helmet on, only the plastic liner. I grabbed that steel pot in a hurry and put it on. I felt somewhat safer, but dreaded the rest of the shelling as we got closer to the shore.

Most of the air power was thrown against warships, especially aircraft carriers. But one troop transport ship, the USS Belinda, a PA, got hit by a suicide plane and only a miracle managed to save her from compartment flooding, explosions, and fires etc. some of the ship's crew were lost aboard her.

J.P. and pals quickly re-entered their familiar routine of shuttling troops, and supplies in and out of the beach. As the front moved inland the shelling ceased and the shore became a relatively safe location. Wanting to see more, J.P., his pal Abernathy and Kruse, their engineer decided to beach the boat and head toward the front and an abandoned Okinawan village—a decision that J.P. would regret. He recounts an encounter that certainly adds to his cumulative level of PTSD qualified events. He shares:

Unknown to me, while I was poking around in one of the houses for souvenirs, Abernathy and the engineer had gone and left me there by myself. I don't know how long I stayed in that dark house poking around the place for souvenirs.

Suddenly I heard a slight noise. I looked toward the door and the tip of a bayonet was stuck inside and as I watched it began to ease in very slowly. Fear ripped through me like a bolt of lightning. My hair stood on end—a damn Jap soldier left behind!

As the bayonet inched in ever so slow I got a battle plan going. I would pussy foot softly and swiftly to position myself just beside the door and as he came in I would spring and try to get inside that bayonet, grab him by the shoulder, draw him up close to me and swiftly stab him through the neck and with the cutting edge of my K-bar knife.

All at once my fear left me and I felt like I had been shot full of some kind of dope. I have never been more alive, more alert in my life. My mental facilities and physical facilities were as finely honed as a razors cutting edge. I started toward the man with the bayonet to take position just inside the door. I was just beginning to enjoy this cat and mouse game of wits.

I was almost to the position I wanted beside the door when he came in with a rush—the bayonet pointed to the wall opposite the door. As he tried to turn, I sprang like a tiger. When I sprang I wouldn't have traded place with any man in the world. I was shot full of adrenaline.

My left hand got him by the shoulder as I had planned. Good! Now I was inside that bayonet. I drew him closer to me and started to drive to his throat with my knife. That man was mine. A surge of pure joy went through me.

All at once I stopped. How I stopped that drive to his throat—I'll never know. Hell, he was an American! I started to kill him anyhow—just for scaring hell out of me. I let him go and backed up a couple of steps— still ready to fight if he wanted to. I was primed to kill and was disappointed as hell because he wasn't the Jap I hoped he was.

Then, I felt weak as water and started shaking. I began to cuss him, I cussed him, his friends, his momma, his daddy, his aunts and uncles, and his shipmates. All the time he just looked at me, never opening his mouth to say a word. After a few moments of my cussing the air 'til it was blue, finally wearily, he walked out of the Okinawan house.

To this day I do not know what his voice sounds like. After he left, I sheathed my knife and walked outside, looking around, thinking about nothing. All at once, while I stood there weakly and exhausted, I started pissing in my britches. I didn't try to stop. I couldn't. I had lost control of my bladder.

This incident, when added to J.P.'s other wartime experiences, clearly qualifies as a probable PTSD producing event. In his next letter to Harold J.P. gives an indication of his trauma and its effect on his memory.

Harold,

A little more about WWII and my adventures in it.

Well, after the episode at the Okinawan house where I experienced the closest thing possible in hand to hand combat I wandered around till much later in the day. I was pretty shaken up and I don't remember too good the things that happened.

On his way back to the shore J.P. and his companions were caught in an artillery exchange. They escaped direct injury, yet experienced the conditions that produced shell shock in World War One. And, he compares the onshore artillery barrage to his experiences being shelled in his boat during landings.

He shares with Harold:

Sometimes a very close miss is something else, the concussion from the explosion slams you in the gut like getting hit in the stomach with a 2x4 timber. Makes you a little sick.

Boats get shot up with sometimes a large hole above the water line you could throw a 55 gallon drum through. Rough! And then the damn infernal screaming, whining shell fragments. All of them, even those going away, sound like they are all coming toward your head. Of course there are plenty of trips in which nothing happens. No shelling, No nothing, just work a plenty. Those are the good trips.

One day I went ashore with a load of ammo, powder charges for 105mm artillery, P.X. supplies, water, and gasoline in 5 gallon cans. Hurrah, I discovered a case of medical grade 190 proof grain alcohol in the cargo. What luck! It was easily identified in a varnished plywood case. I opened a P.X. case of supplies which contained 17 cartons of cigarettes. We took all the Camels, Luckys and Chesterfields, and nailed the Chelseas, Sir Walter Raleighs back into the case. We took two quarts of medical alcohol, too. Mixed it with grapefruit juice. It turned the juice as white as milk. All of us in the surrounding boats which were tied up on the beach together got about drunk. A bunch of us went swimming during an air raid in which 12 Jap planes were shot down in the area around us. What a hell of a party. Boy what a kick that raw grain alcohol had. Wow! Indeed!

CHAPTER TWENTY-ONE

Victory at Okinawa, the End of the War, and Getting Out

Harold,

The Japanese fleet, or what was left of it, never showed up at Okinawa. A lot of the Jap ships had been sunk or badly damaged. Some of it was under repair in Japanese shipyards and was subject to further damage by B-29 bombers from Iwo Jima and Tinian. Daily bombing raids were hitting many parts of Japan. The once renowned and much feared battle fleet was no more. The Jap navy was finis.

The Jap Air Force was short of planes, spare parts, and gasoline and especially experienced pilots. It was fast being obliterated as an effective fighting force. Its days were numbered.

Finally, the day came when we received orders to depart Okinawa. We made preparations to get underway and said goodbye to Okinawa as we set sail to God knows where.

A MONG THOSE SPOTS ONLY KNOWN TO THE MOST high where the *Fuller* would go were the Admiralty Islands of Alaska, French Indo-China (Vietnam) and later China, which included shuttling Chinese nationalist troops from French Indo-China to Tiensen on the Chinese mainland.

So night and day we sailed on, up and down to our usual tactics: crap games, work, watches at night, and politicking the cooks for food, and as usual, stealing it when the opportunity presented itself. Just a bunch of good ole thieving, politicking sea lawyers, asphalt Arabs, and ole salty dogs. We sinned on joyfully.

The grinding routine of sea duty was not monolithic and the war had its ebbs and flows. The drudgery of routine could be broken by the imaginations and antics of the youths who made up the crew.

A lot of the time we were at sea or at anchor considerable ways from the war, so we could feel reasonably safe to carry on our work and take care of the business of living at sea.

Days were full and busy but we engaged in horseplay now and then. Sometimes when at anchor we jumped over the sides of the ship and went swimming. Nobody considered sharks a danger— never heard of anyone being attacked by one.

Men just out of boyhood also found mischievous things to do.

We stole about everything that wasn't nailed down. Even if it had a guard posted over it we would find a way to steal Army and Marine Corps beer.

****

We were a thieving, conniving bunch of ole sea dogs. So salty we had wrung more salt water out of our socks than most landlubbers ever saw. Man, that's salty! All ole sea dogs are salty as all get out. Ask any sea going sailor. The first thing he'll tell you is how salty he is. Ha ha.

Some of us got liberty to go in to the city for a few drinks and recreation and especially to buy high quality silk kimonos, which cost about 20,000 Yuan, only about $10 in an exchange rate that was 1,800 Yuan to the dollar.

Lots of boats and Chinese peddling jewelry, watches, and other items came out to the ship. I bought several quart bottles of whiskey for $2.00 per bottle. We could get wine or whiskey almost any time we wanted it from the Chinese merchants in boats. A dollar would buy a lot of rice or whiskey and other stuff in North China.

Upon hearing that the war was over J.P. and his pals were elated. The reason they had enlisted had been fulfilled:

Everyone in the ship's crew was overjoyed. Hell, we were almost civilians already! Outside of work, we considered only a few things worth talking about, one was thievery, goldbricking, food, and women, and of course beer. We all sat around shooting the bull and laying great plans to be implemented when we were discharged back into civilian life. Everyone wanted out of the Navy yesterday, or tomorrow at the latest.

When finally ordered home J.P. and his shipmates celebrated as usual, with a party that naturally centered upon drinking.

The news spread and the whole crew got into a bottle that night and got drunk.

Again, J.P. honestly and succinctly shares his appraisal of one of the pastimes of ordinary seamen...

We stole everything that wasn't nailed down.

CHAPTER TWENTY-TWO

"Decommissioning" the Sailor Man

W HILE IN THE SEATTLE AREA, WAITING TO DECOMMISSION the *Fuller*, J.P. ferried sailors to and from the city and falls deeper in the clutches of alcohol and other, more serious numbing agents. His actions to seek relief even escalated to the theft of surplus drugs.

Me and my crew were kept busy, bringing liberty parties back to the Fuller, *sometimes taking them to Squamish (Washington) to catch the ferry. I got lots of liberty myself, spending the night in some hotel in Seattle going from tavern to tavern. He laments: Only beer and wine at those watering holes.*

The days passed and we were to be decommissioned before long. Already the personnel in sick bay were setting out cases and cases of drugs. Morphine Sulphate ¼ grain in syringes were setting everywhere. I found 2 ounces of pure cocaine and hid it along with some morphine. One day the place was ate up with Customs Inspector. They didn't find the dope I had hidden, but

*it scared me, so one night late I took the stuff and
threw it overboard.*

By this time J.P.'s use of alcohol has escalated to the point
where it has invaded all aspects of life—even relations with his
immediate family. When arriving home for a thirty day leave,
alcohol is his homecoming gift for the family.

*I was home with 4 bottles of whiskey and a half pint
of pure corn whiskey.*

At home J.P focused a great deal on alcohol, becoming
somewhat of a homespun connoisseur:

*Moonshine whiskey was $3.00 per pint and some of
it was made out of sorghum syrup and potatoes.
Some of it tasted like shit, but it got you high as a
Georgia pine without poisoning you. There were
different kinds, some of it was fighting whiskey and
some of it was O'possum hunting whiskey, and with
some of the stuff you could chase women for days
with a gallon of the stuff and a few bites of food until
you would completely give out. I prefer the women
chasing kind, ha ha.*

J.P. returned to Washington State for the *Fuller's* decom-
missioning and his own release from duty.

*Finally the day came when we put on our best shined
shoes and dress uniforms and attended the decom-
missioning ceremony. Scott, Boson's Mate 2nd Class,*

piped the flag down after the ceremony and as a navy ship the Fuller *ceased to exist.*

It was a sad moment, the death of the good ship Fuller. *I was choked up like the rest of the small crew. Later that day we disembarked the ship for the last time ever. All of us had heavy hearts for that good ole ship had been home to us for many months. It was almost like a mother dying.*

J.P. is sent back home again on a second thirty day leave to wait on final processing and his release from active duty. Again, he arrives home with alcohol as his homecoming gift. This time it was four bottles, minus the half pint of corn liquor.

A few days later I arrived back home with four quarts of good bonded whiskey. I really began to enjoy things. I had 60 days leave in the past 6 months.

After a booze-filled leave he reports to a New Orleans, Louisiana naval facility where...

I drew my pay for the 30 day leave and meal tickets' pay. For a few days I had nothing to do but drink.

...and performs lowly guard duty to protect female staff (WAVES) and drinks a lot waiting for his release. Finally, one day...

Then came the word that we were to be sent to

Millington Naval Air Station near Memphis for discharge. To celebrate, I drank a belly full of beer, got about half drunk, bid some friends goodbye, and packed my suit case for the trip.

The next day or two we were processed like when we first joined the service. They sent Savage and me to a couple of shrinks (psychiatrists). They questioned us about this and that. We were reluctant to talk about anything regarding the war or naval service or anything of a serious nature. To them this was good. They gave us a clean bill of health.

The Navy should have asked questions to learn of concerns which would have long term effects on veterans. Concerns from situations such as the multiple occasions in combat where J.P. had worked well past the point of exhaustion.

J.P. recounts a time at Okinawa:

Time went by while we worked days and nights. I lost track of time. Sleep was an overwhelming compulsion. A 20-30 minute doze was very refreshing. Lord, what I would give for just two hours of sleep without having to wake up and go to work.

I had been on duty without relief 4 full days, and almost 3 nights. I was literally dead. The whole crew was. Then on the 4th evening they sent a relief engineer. Did they relieve me? Hell no!

Anyhow the new engineer was fresh and I turned the operation of the boat to him. I'm about dead. I told him, "I'm on my very last legs and I've got to get an hour or so sleep." We were laying off the starboard side of the USS DuPage waiting to start loading. "If you get the signal to load, wake me," I told the relief engineer.

Before he came aboard I had gone without sleep so long that I was having mild hallucinations. Little gold specks and something like ground up brown leaves were floating down like rain before my eyes. I would get silly and giggle aloud. I sailed a biscuit from a bread ration at the officer of the deck on the DuPage. I thought it was funny. That kind of funny business could get me in trouble.

I got a wet blanket and lay down in the well of the boat and in a minute I was sound asleep. I awoke a little later when something jarred the boat all to hell. I stood up. A Jap plane had bombed a tug boat and oil barge about 200 yards ahead of us. As I watched the ships around me shoot him down, another one was flying around. They shot and shot and shot some more with the big AA guns and couldn't knock him down. After about five or ten minutes I got disgusted and said to hell with him and went back to sleep, him still buzzing around,

I awoke a little after dark feeling good and refreshed. Hell, I must have got a good three hours sleep. I felt fine and wonder of wonders they sent a relief crew, except the engineer. The relief coxswain took us back to the ship. Everybody was talking about the big air raid. "The big air raid?" I said. "Hell, what big air raid? Only air raid I saw was two planes buzzing around trying to do a little damage."

Come to find out. The Japs had sent an estimated 455 planes in an attack that evening, and we, the convoy, had shot down an estimated 385 of them. The ship got 2 and a half. What a hell of a way to spend an evening! Slept all through it!

****

The Navy also should have had concerns related to the accumulated effect of the constant fear of being torpedoed. For sailors like J.P. it was very real:

When I stood the 4 to 8 watch each morning, I had to take the Union Jack, a little flag with stars and no stripes, and mount it on the bow of the ship. One day I was mounting it and about 100 feet ahead of the ship two torpedoes streaked by, one slightly behind the other, streaming bubbles like all get out. My heart jumped into my mouth. Too late to give any warning—they had already passed!

They were two of the three torpedoes that I saw pass by narrowly missing the ship. There may have been others. There probably were. I considered ourselves damn lucky after such a close call. After the watch I could sleep a little late in the mornings. Lots of the cause for loss of sleep was caused by having to stay at General Quarters so much at night.

The Japs harassed us with small inefficient air raids often only consisting of a couple of observation planes. I think they harassed us at night by flying planes into radar range and doing nothing but keeping us at battle stations so much at night that we were nothing but zombies from lack of sleep.

And, there should have been concerns about the inhumanity of war and what it can do to the basic sensibilities of participants. During one hellish night of sweltering sleep deprived duty, J.P. shares:

It was so hot that I slept on the deck. On one occasion I rolled a dead marine out of a stretcher and slept in it. I put him back in the next morning no worse for wear.

So much for the recruiting pamphlet's boast of, "solid comfort" in a comfortable "spring bunk."

One can only ask, how is a teenager's mind affected by such circumstances? The answer may be found in J.P.'s reaction to decorations for service and bravery. When headed home the last time he writes:

By this time, we had been authorized another bronze battle star on our Asiatic-Pacific ribbon. I got out my campaign ribbons and looked at them. The Asiatic-Pacific ribbon had four stars already. The Philippine Liberation ribbon had two.

Five stars on one ribbon made me an "ace." I could wear a silver star instead five bronze ones. I purchased the little silver star at the canteen, took off the four bronze ones and solemnly mounted the silver one.

I regarded the decoration with some distaste. We almost never wore them, too much like bragging. There were times we were ordered to wear them. We promptly took them off when we reached shore. It seemed a little sacrilegious to wear them boastfully while so many of our fallen comrades were still fresh in our memories.

I kept them, took them with me, but almost never wore them except while I wore my dress blues at home on leave. Four medals, ribbons, and seven battle stars were an impressive decoration on any uniform, but sadly they gave me no real pride or satisfaction. Too many of our comrades in arms would never wear theirs and walk the streets again. Occasionally I said a little for prayer them, sometimes with a tear or two in the corner of my eyes. I regard them all as better men than I would ever be.

The Navy gave sailors clean bills of health because it suited the situation. The war was over and it was time to move on. Little regard was given to those suffering with and changed by PTSD.

J.P. gives additional somber testimony on how the war changed him:

I still sat around at night in deep thought and others did, too. I thought of the numerous good men who had died themselves. Better and braver men than I would ever be. I felt guilty just because I was alive, and sometimes I felt like there would be peace in my heart only if I joined them in death. Slowly, I lost part of the will to live and later I didn't much give a damn whether I lived or died.

Upon his release and final trip home, a still teenaged J.P.—filled with doubt and despair—resorted to what had become familiar behavior.

I got off the bus in Memphis, had a few drinks for the road and bought a goodly supply of whiskey, and late that night caught a train for Birmingham which would put me close to home. The next day I walked into home. Everyone talked at once. Mama was ironing with a kerosene iron, she was grinning from ear to ear. My oldest sister Audrey was having a fit.

I opened a bottle and offered everyone a drink then took one myself. I offered a toast to them and to the Navy. I said, "Well, I'm home and I want you all to know, I love the hell out of you people," and I grinned at them and said, "and this booze, too."

Goodbye—END

For the adult J.P., and in his memory, this was the end of his naval experience. However, for the nineteen-year-old returning veteran, early 1946 was not the end. It was actually just the beginning of the end—his.

SAILOR MAN

CHAPTER TWENTY-THREE

Home

J.P. HAD A PROBLEM. THE WIDELY BELOVED Alabama farm boy was no more, and the "Sailor Man" of his dreams would never be. Alcohol had become his best friend, and its abuse was a clear sign of PTSD. However, the malady's link to alcoholism was not widely understood at the time, and essentially, unrecognized. PTSD, also known as Estar Roto, means "to be broken." For J.P. the outcome of his illegal enlistment and devotion of his final teen years to the war was that he indeed was broken.

For the alcohol dependent nineteen-year-old veteran the question was simple: Could he build a new life? The answer was not so clear. Being at home elevated J.P.'s thoughts and he was optimistic:

Things were really looking up for me. I was a civilian again. I had spent 2 years at sea, most of the time under way always going somewhere. The question was could I settle down?

J.P. earnestly tried to make a go of it. At home with his parents, he found employment at the Bemiston Cotton Mill

J.P. a few years after the war, and before hard times hit.

and attempted to construct a normal civilian life. But, as his sister Audrey shared, "After the war J.P. was just not the same person. He held on for some years, but the alcohol was the thing that sent him down. It began right away, in 1946." Between drinking bouts J.P. pursued Gladys Louise Baker, and in 1950 they were wed. The following year the couple welcomed son, Harold, into their world.

J.P. forthrightly shared with Harold how the question of his settling down finally was resolved:

The answer became apparent later on after I married your mother. Hell, I just disappointed that woman very much and I'm sorry if I ever hurt her— even one time—because I loved her very very much. At the time I think she loved me, too. She stood by me in some miserable days.

Those days began when J.P. displayed behavior at work that would later be described as a nervous breakdown. Audrey explained that J.P. "flipped out," in reaction to the ever present noise that was a constant characteristic in such facilities. Sensitivity to noise, particularly the incessant and repetitive variety found in cotton mills, is a leading triggering mechanism for symptoms of post-traumatic stress disorder. J.P. could not bear the noise of his workplace and finally broke. The result was that he was hospitalized and treated through the application of electro-shock therapy.

J.P. recalls the episode:

I didn't have enough sense to get out of that rotten hell hole of Bemiston Cotton Mill.

After his discharge from the hospital the downward spiral accelerated. J.P. retreated into himself. Audrey shared that, "From then on, J.P. could never stand to be enclosed." And,

"He always rubbed his head, as if he was being shocked again and again."

The treatment was ineffective. What followed was a second hospitalization, more shock therapy, a divorce, the handing over of his son to relatives to care for and raise him, and, of course, the continued abuse of alcohol.

Harold explained what the family shared with him about his father at the time: "Everyone said he was not the same person. Too young, and not prepared for war; he was not a fighter, or a violent person. He became self-centered and told them very little. All he talked about was how terrible it was to see what the boys looked like coming back on the boats. That and the terrible air raids is all he shared."

Audrey stated that military service deeply and sorely affected her brother and replaced a life of promise with an endless cycle of odd jobs, drinking bouts, arrests and jail. She lamented, "Maybe if he had talked about what had happened to him things would have been better." In support of his aunt's point of view, Harold observed, "In my opinion the drink was a method of killing himself."

Conceding his fate and giving-in to alcohol was how J.P. ultimately dealt with his condition. In one brief truthful admission, J.P. summarized his life to Harold:

I don't think I had a dog's chance.

J.P. fell into the downward spiral initiated by his PTSD. The drinking escalated and so did his erratic behavior. He ranted, raved, and catapulted furniture in acts of violence not aimed at anyone, but instead "just was out of his head" and mad at the world. On one occasion he almost burned the house down with a tossed lamp. He held no job longer than six months. For the

Harold Nunnally, J.P.'s son and recipient of his letters, is a successful businessman and retired Army Reserve Officer, residing in Huntsville, Alabama.

small remnant of the once patriotic Sixteen-Year-Old Sailor Man there would be no G.I. Bill, no promising career, and no ranch house in the suburbs. Odd jobs and living with friends and relatives, as long as they could bear him, was how he would spend his life, a life away from his son.

On one occasion during his correspondence to Harold, J.P. diverted from his narrative to send a gift. Perhaps it was his way to make up for the years he was not around. It was as

J.P. at the time of his correspondence with Harold.

if he wished to portray a side that was less embittered and not addicted to drink. After sending a copy of a samurai sword he wrote Harold:

> *I saw several during the war. I might have traded or bought one or more of them for $50, or less, but I did not, as they were only souvenirs not thought of too highly at the time. The true samurai sword was handed down from father to son for generations.*

They were a family heirloom among samurai warriors. Some of the swords were hundreds of years old. After the war the Japanese families started to try to buy back many of the captured swords. They were willing to pay a fancy price for them. I do not think there are many of them left in collector's and private hands. If you could locate one it would probably cost thousands.

I have never seen one in civilian life. It has a certain type of beauty all right. Like the sleek dark beauty of a battle ship or the deadly coiled sleek beauty of a deadly striking rattlesnake. The aura of death and destruction hangs over things of this nature—doomsday.

Prophetically, J.P. says:

It should serve to teach us a lesson.

It is a stark lesson to be preached by a man who would, perhaps in jest and perhaps not, end a letter with a sad "disclaimer" for being a drinker:

P.S. Took your advice and took the twenty and got some wine. Ha ha, I'm one up on you boy, instead of getting one bottle of good wine, I got three bottles of cheap wine. So I feel 3 times as good ha ha, as you can tell from this drunk ass letter.

And a second, longer disclaimer:

Be good and take care, Write, Love Pa-J.P.
P.S. Thanks for the $20 you sent for Xmas. Pay no

attention to that shitty letter I wrote. I was both about sick and drunk as 700 hells when I wrote. Forgive me ole buddy. Luck in everything you undertake. "Drink wine makes you feel fine" ha ha J.P. Nunnally-owned and operated by the Blatz brewing C.-Milwaukee Wisc. Guaranteed alcohol content 5% by volume.

And a third, which aches with as much pain as any observer could imagine:

Thanks for the $20 you sent for Xmas. You asked me to think of you on Xmas. I got drunk, but there hasn't been many days since you were kicking around in your mama's belly that I haven't thought of you, worried about you and wished you the very best in everything you do. I still do. Wish I had done more.

Love to all, your pa, J.P.

CHAPTER TWENTY-FOUR

Was It Worth It?

I N THE PROCESS OF ANSWERING THE QUESTION, "What happened?" J.P. summarized his experiences in war with graphic and blunt honesty. At Harold's request J.P. set about the task earnestly and he held nothing back in peeling back the layers of his personal onion of pain. In each letter J.P. revealed the events and forces that forever transformed an idealistic, patriotic teenager into a man saturated in alcohol and haunted by the torment of war.

From a vantage point more than four decades distant to the events he described, J.P. the man, is anything but a blindly patriotic boy. There can be no more dramatic, complete, and deep-felt turnaround than when he shares:

One day you believe in God and pray to him, and the next day, after you see a good honest decent man's guts running out his body you want to shit in God's face.

J.P. remained on the edge of patriotic sacrilege and shared:

*Well, Harold, the whole scoop. War is nothing but a
goddamn insane asylum with honest decent brave
men running the damn asylum. A nothing, the pits,
the shits, the only glory is in the minds of a bunch of
fools writing how wonderful a bunch of shit is.*

Yet, even with such a strong and clearly negative opinion
about war, J.P. still assessed his time in the Navy with no
whining. He made no direct connection between his alcohol
abuse and having experienced traumatic events in service to
his country. In his view he served, came home, and had bad
luck. J.P. remained a Sailor Man to the very end and simply
summarized his WWII service as follows:

Harold,

*Hope you can make some sense out of the war stories
I've been sending you. It's been such a long time since
all that happened. As for me, the work I done, as well
as my shipmates, was the most important thing.*

It is not known how many teenagers lied, altered their birth
dates, or assumed false identities in order to serve their country
during World War Two. The peak year for such activity was 1943,
the year of J.P.'s enlistment, and, unlike him, nearly 50,000
fraudulent service members were detected and sent home.
However, a much larger number, perhaps as many as 200,000
went undetected and served honorably, as did J.P. Among those
who eventually managed to enlist and bravely serve, a few were
discovered, court-martialed, and relieved of their medals. No one
knows the number that suffered from PTSD, survived combat-
related wounds, or even how many died in combat.

A collection of J.P's various medals. J.P. had a change of heart and ordered his awards, delivering them to Harold for safekeeping.

The following quote contains much for us to contemplate in considering J.P.'s sacrifice. It is from *Children at War: Underage Americans Illegally Fighting in the Second World War*, by Joshua R. Pollarine:

> They left their schools, their friends, and their families, with ideals of adventure and excitement, to defend their nation and their homes. They soon learned the truth of war. Their experiences were beyond anything they could have imagined in their youthful dreams of glory. For all of them, the realities of war rapidly distilled any romantic notions of what defending America truly meant. They

lost close friends, saw horrors that would haunt them throughout their lives, and suffered the devastating effects of combat on the body.

From the dawn of armed conflict, children and teenagers have been recruited to serve in the military, and although the practice is rarer today, it sadly still exists. Yet, even when it is prompted by flag-waving patriotism and widely accepted, as was the case in WWII, the question must be asked of the practice—is it worth it? Accounts such as J.P.'s clearly reveal that the answer is, "No." And when weighed against the available services of more than sixteen million men and women that the United States placed in uniform during World War Two, the practice was not even necessary.

CHAPTER TWENTY-FIVE

The Sailor Man's Goodbye

J.P. NUNNALLY DIED ON JULY 29, 1994. In anticipation of the event he purchased a $3,000 insurance policy, payable to Harold as his beneficiary. J.P.'s grave is simply marked with a standard veteran's headstone, which of course makes no reference to his disability, his under-aged service, nor the lost potential of his life.

Similar to his letters, and in his own direct and honest style, J.P. penned the following poem of farewell, as if in apology for his unproductive life. It is clear that he merely wished to be remembered as one who tried and failed, but meant well:

THE LAST ROUND UP FOR OLE J.P.

I say, Goodbye, bye, bye, bye
To the family God gave me.
When I draw my pay
On Judgment Day
Please don't speak against me.

SAILOR MAN

We one and all
Shall surely fall,
It's the will of God we do.
Forgiveness is the song of life.
God's word says it's true.
My heart is heavy.
My soul is naught.
My sins weigh upon me greatly.
My son is grown,
Doing fine on his own,
Though, I have not seen him lately.
To Louise:
He's a fine young man
And he is half you and me.
We done some good
As I knew we would
When we slipped behind that tree.
The grass was green.
The time was right.
Our love was strong.
T'was a good night.
The good Lord must have smiled a bit,
As a candle in the soul
Of an infant was lit.
To All:
With these parting words
I leave you to be
A judge of the character
Of little ole me.
As a little man
I'm afraid it's true,

One that never
Carried his weight too good,
Though sometimes I thought
Maybe I could.
The strong shall perish.
The weak shall fall.
Only the love of God
Can save us all.
Peace.
Peace and forgiveness,
Before I go.
Peace to everyone I know.
Amen.
J.P.

SAILOR MAN

AUTHOR'S COMMENTS

MY PURPOSE IN WRITING *SAILOR MAN* WAS THREEFOLD: to honor J.P.'s sacrificial service to his country, to facilitate closure for the Nunnally family, and to recognize the contributions of all who served in World War Two as under-aged enlistees. *Sailor Man* is my "thank you" to them. Additionally, I wish to thank Harold Nunnally for sharing J.P.'s letters, giving me the opportunity to present another story from the USS *Fuller*.

SAILOR MAN

APPENDIX

Abbreviations Used for Certain Landing Boats and Ships in Amphibious Operations

Ships and boats designed especially for amphibious operations are listed below. They appear in order of size from largest to smallest in length.

Abbreviation	Type
LSD	Landing Ship Dock
LST	Landing Ship Tank
LSM	Landing Ship Medium
LSI(L)	Landing Ship Infantry (Large)
LCT	Landing Craft Tank
LCC	Landing Craft Control
LCM	Landing Craft Mechanized
LCVP	Landing Craft Vehicle Personnel
LCV	Landing Craft Vehicle
LCPR	Landing Craft Personnel with ramp
LCP(L)	Landing Craft Personnel (Large)
LCS	Landing Craft Support
LVT	Landing Vehicle Tracked
LCR	Landing Craft Rubber

Ships which support amphibious operations but which were not originally designed for seaborne attack, include those below. They are given in order of length.

Abbreviation	Type
CV	Aircraft Carrier
BB	Battleship
CA	Heavy Cruiser
CL	Light Cruiser
AO	Oiler
CVE	Escort Aircraft Carrier
APA	Attack Transport
AKA	Attack Cargo Ship
DD	Destroyer
DE	Destroyer escort
SS	Submarine
AM	Minesweeper
AK	Cargo Ship
AP	Transport

ABOUT THE AUTHOR

D EL STAECKER, FELLOW OF THE ROYAL SOCIETY OF ARTS, is a 1972 graduate of The Citadel, The Military College of South Carolina. He is the author of *The Lady Gangster: A Sailor's Memoir*, the multiple award winning account of the USS *Fuller*, WWII's *Queen of Attack Transports*. In 2012 he was named a U.S. Navy "Writer on Deck" and in 2013 was a finalist for Author of the Year for the Military Writers Society of America.

Made in the USA
Charleston, SC
13 April 2015